The Torch of Certainty

The Torch of Certainty

Jamgon Kongtrul the Great

Translated from the Tibetan by Judith Hanson

Foreword by Chögyam Trungpa

Shambhala

Boston & London • *2000*

SHAMBHALA PUBLICATIONS, INC.
Horticultural Hall
300 Massachusetts Avenue
Boston, Massachusetts 02115
www.shambhala.com

⊗ Printed in the United States of America
Distributed in the United States by Random
House, Inc., and in Canada by Random House of
Canada Ltd

LIBRARY OF CONGRESS CATALOGING-IN-PUBLICATION DATA
Koṅ-sprul Blo-gros-mtha'-yas, 1813–1899.
    The torch of certainty.

    Translation of Ñes don sgron me
    Reprint. Originally published: Boulder, Colo.:
Shambhala, 1977.
    Bibliography: p.
    Includes index.
    1. Meditation (Tantric Buddhism.)   2. Kar-ma-pa
(Sect.)—Liturgy—Texts.   I. Hanson, Judith.
II. Title.
BQ7805.K6613   1983   294.3'443   82-24522
ISBN 1-57062-713-4 (pbk.)

BVG 01

TO KALU RINPOCHE, beloved Lama

*who has urged that practice of the Four Special Foundations
be preceded by ritual authorization to use the texts (lung), one
Vajrayana empowerment (wong), and a Lama's instructions (tri).
These will inform your practice and contribute to its success.*

Contents

Illustrations

Foreword

The spirituality of Buddhism is a nontheistic one. It deals with the ways and means of attaining enlightenment, discovering Buddha within through the aid of great teachers and the diligent practice of meditation. It has always been emphasized that one does not purely practice the Dharma, but one becomes the Dharma.

The teachings of Buddha are divided into three sections: Hinayana, Mahayana, and Vajrayana. They should be methodically practiced in this order. If one does not begin at the beginning, there is a danger of provoking further confusion, of viewing practice as entertainment, which only causes greater arrogance and neurosis.

The pattern of the practitioner's progress through the three yanas is as follows: First, one develops extreme exertion in uncovering one's own neurosis. This one-pointed mindfulness brings the sense of one's actual human quality. The second stage is marked by gentleness, allowing one's energies to expand and be shared with the rest of sentient beings. Finally, one develops fearlessness and a sense of joy and penetrating insight, filled with immense devotion to the lineage and one's root-guru. This text, dealing with the preliminary practices of the Vajrayana discipline, belongs to the third category.

I am very pleased that this authentic torch of certainty is available to those who are inspired to follow the Vajrayana path. It was written by Jamgon Kongtrul the Great, whose reincarnation, Jamgon Kongtrul of Zhe-chen, was my root-guru. Those who are deeply inspired by this book should receive oral transmission from a living lineage-holder. They should have a strong foundation in Hinayana and Mahayana as a prelude to entering the path of Vajrayana. This is the way which has been taught.

Judith Hanson has put a great deal of energy and devotion into the translation of this text. The fruition of her effort is evidence of her karmic link with the Kagyud tradition.

Vajracarya the Venerable Chögyam Trungpa
March 1, 1977

Preface

Jamgon Kongtrul's *The Torch of Certainty (Nges-don sgron-me)* is a text of great importance to students of Buddhism because it deals with a set of basic meditative practices in current use by all Tibetan sects. These are the "Four Foundations" or preliminary practices *(sngon-'gro)*.

This annotated translation of *Nges-don sgron-me* is preceded by two introductory chapters. The first contains some historical background on the text, the author and his sect, the Karma Kagyudpa. The second contains a description of the general procedures for practice of the Four Foundations, as well as transcripts of interviews with three leading Lamas (Venerable Kalu Rinpoche, Venerable Deshung Rinpoche and Venerable Chögyam Trungpa, Rinpoche), who answer the questions of a prospective practitioner.

Each chapter of the translation is preceded by further introductory remarks. The introductions to chapters 2 through 5 contain detailed instructions for practice. These were given by Kalu Rinpoche and his representative Lama Tsengyur Rinpoche (Tsewong Gyurme) at Kagyu Kunkhyab Chuling in Vancouver.

Throughout the text non-English terms in parentheses are trans-literations of the Tibetan, unless otherwise noted.

Frequently cited in the notes are the comments of four authorita-tive Tibetan informants: Kalu Rinpoche, Tsengyur Rinpoche, Deshung Rinpoche and Lobsang P. Lhalungpa. Through their responses to my questions at numerous interviews, these men provided traditional oral commentary which made the text intelligible to me and made its trans-lation possible. A biographical sketch of each of these Tibetans will shed light on their contributions.

The Venerable Kalu Rinpoche, one of several contemporary in-carnations of Jamgon Kongtrul, is a meditation master of both the Shangpa and Karma branches of the Kagyud sect. He is one of the few refugee Lamas fully trained in Tibet. Born in Kham (eastern Tibet) in 1904, he was educated by his father until the age of sixteen. Thereafter, his principal teacher was Lama Norbu Dondrub, a pupil of Jamgon Kongtrul. At twenty-five, Rinpoche began twelve years of intensive

meditation in an isolated retreat. Subsequently, he was in charge of the
meditation center at Kongtrul's former monastery of Palpung for fifteen
years. There he guided monks in the Four Foundations and more advanced practices such as the Six Yogas of Naropa. In the late 1950's he
fled to Bhutan and established a monastery. Five years later he moved to
northern India and founded Samdub Tarjay (bSam-'grub Thar-byed)
monastery at Sonada, where he now supervises more than thirty monks
in meditation.

While touring Europe and North America in 1972 and 1974-5,
Rinpoche established approximately thirty Buddhist centers. During his
visit to Vancouver, he left his disciple Lama Tsewong Gyurme as meditation teacher and spiritual guide of the newly founded Kagyu Kunkhyab
Chuling.

Lama Tsewong Gyurme (abbreviated "Lama" or "the Lama" in the
following chapters) was born in Kham in 1939. He received his primary
education at a Karma Kagyud monastery, but at sixteen went to Zhe-
chen, the Nyingma monastery where Jamgon Kongtrul received his original monastic vows. There he was ordained and studied the philosophical
works of the renowned Nyingma scholar Lama Mipham (1846-1912).
At nineteen he fled to Bhutan where he lived and worked at Kalu
Rinpoche's monastery for five years. He followed Rinpoche to India in
1963. With the founding of Samdub Tarjay monastery in Sonada, Tsewong Gyurme was able to pursue his lifelong ambition of intensive
meditative practice. Soon after his completion of the traditional three
year meditation retreat, at Kalu Rinpoche's request he came to Canada.
Since 1972 he has been instructing students at Kagyu Kunkhyab Chuling
in the fundamental tenets of Buddhism, the meditation on Avalokiteshvara (sPyan-ras-gzigs), the Four Foundations and other basic practices.

During His Holiness the Karmapa's visit to Vancouver in 1974, he
gave Tsewong Gyurme the title "Cho kyi Lama" (chos-kyi bla-ma, "es-
teemed religious teacher") in recognition of his teaching accomplishments. His Holiness announced that the Lama was henceforth to be
known as Tsengyur Rinpoche and be head Lama to all of Kalu Rinpoche's
North American centers.

The Venerable Deshung Rinpoche,[1] profound eclectic scholar of
the Sakya sect, was born in Kham in 1906. From the age of three, he

---

1. Much of the biographical information on Deshung Rinpoche was
kindly provided by his Seattle Mahayana center, Sakya Thegchen Choling.

lived with his uncle Lama Ngawong Nyima during the last five years of
the latter's fifteen year meditation retreat. There he memorized the songs
of Milarepa.

At age eight, Rinpoche went to Tharlam monastery and was ordained. Both the head of the Sakya sect and Tharlam's abbot, the renowned meditation master Ngawong Lepa Rinpoche (dGa'-ston Ngag-
dbang Legs-pa, 1864-1941), officially recognized him as the Deshung
tulku,[2] incarnation of Lama Lungrig Nyima, abbot of Deshung monastery.

Until he was seventeen, Rinpoche studied at Tharlam with Ngawong
Lepa. He then stayed at Deshung for two years. He returned to Tharlam,
but was soon sent by Ngawong Lepa to further his studies in the Dege
(sDe-dge) area of Kham. There he studied with more than thirty eminent Lamas of all sects, including Shanphan Chokyi nangwa (gZhan-
phan Chos-kyi snang-ba, 1871-1927), the Khyentse Rinpoche Jamyang
Chokyi lodro ('Jam-dbyangs Chos-kyi blo-gros, 1896-1959) and the
Kongtrul Rinpoche. As a result, he is authorized to teach not only the
advanced meditation practice of the Sakya sect, called Lamdray (Lam-
'bras, "Path and Result"), but also those of the Gelug, Kagyud and
Nyingma sects. Rinpoche rounded off these years of study with a year
in retreat, meditating on Manjushri.

Of all his illustrious teachers, Deshung Rinpoche still considers his
first teacher Ngawong Lepa to be his root-guru, or chief spiritual teacher.
From Ngawong Lepa he received all the empowerments for practices
concerned with the key Sakya yidam Hevajra, the Lamdray teachings
and the complete transmission of the Sakya sect. Shortly before his death,
Ngawong Lepa named Rinpoche his successor as abbot of Tharlam.

For the next ten years Rinpoche toured Kham and gave teachings
and empowerments to thousands of monks. At age forty-four he returned to Tharlam for five years. Following a two year meditation retreat, in 1959 he fled to Lhasa, Bhutan and India. Two years later he
settled in the United States, and taught at the University of Washington.
Following his retirement, he continued his private studies for a few
years. But at age sixty-seven, inspired by the memory of Ngawong Lepa
and by the accomplishments of Kalu Rinpoche in North America, he
emerged from retirement to begin a new teaching career. Since then he
has delivered numerous public lectures and given teachings and empowerments at Kagyu Kunkhyab Chuling in Vancouver. In 1974 he and

2. For discussion of the meaning of tulku, see chap. 2, n. 27.

Sakya Dagchen Rinpoche founded Sakya Thegchen Choling in Seattle, where both serve as resident teachers.

Deshung Rinpoche is currently working with Lobsang P. Lhalungpa on a translation of Dagpo Trashi Namgyal's *Nges-don phyag-rgya-chen-po sgom-rim legs-bshad zla-ba'i 'od-zer* for the Institute for Advanced Studies of World Religions.

Lobsang Phuntsok Lhalungpa (abbreviated "LPL" in the following chapters) was born of a noble family in Lhasa, 1926. His father was Tibet's chief state oracle. After ten years in primary and secondary school, in 1941 he joined the Dalai Lama's government, in which he held several administrative posts. During his ten years of government service, he was engaged in intensive private study of a vast range of philosophical and meditative texts with eminent Lamas of a variety of sects, including his own, the Gelugpa.

From 1947-51 he was the Tibetan government's Cultural and Educational Representative in New Delhi. With his Bhutanese wife Deki, he settled in India and taught Tibetan language, history, culture and religion at several educational institutions.

From 1956-70 he ran the newly created Tibetan section of All-India Radio, where he wrote, directed and read Tibetan language programs on religion, history, music and drama.

In the mid-1960's he was commissioned by the government of Sikkim and by the Dalai Lama's government-in-exile to draw up a curriculum of Tibetan primary education, for which he wrote and co-authored two textbook series.

Mr. Lhalungpa has written or co-authored several works on the arts and language of Tibet and has assisted such eminent Western scholars as G. N. Roerich, R. A. Stein and D. S. Ruegg in research and translation. Both privately and on the Dalai Lama's behalf, he has founded or directed several educational, cultural and craft organizations for Tibetan refugees in India.

In 1971 he moved to Vancouver, where he has taught Tibetan language at the University of British Columbia, helped Tibetan refugees to settle in Canada and continued his private studies. Recently he has contributed to a group retranslation of Milarepa's biography under the direction of Dr. Jacob Needleman, published by Dutton, and translated a group of texts on intellectual discipline (*blo-sbyong*). Mr. Lhalungpa is currently translating Dagpo Trashi Namgyal's Mahamudra text *Nges-don phyag-rgya-chen-po sgom-rim legs-bshad zla-ba'i 'od-zer,* to be published by the Institute for Advanced Studies of World Religions.

ACKNOWLEDGEMENTS

I wish to thank Dr. Shotaro Iida (University of British Columbia) for suggesting translation of this text as my M.A. thesis, and Professor J. I. Richardson for the unwavering confidence and support with which he guided me to its completion.

I am especially grateful to the Venerable Kalu Rinpoche, Kagyudpa meditation master and teacher, for his invaluable comments on lineage, doctrine and practice, for his authorization to use the text, and most of all, for the enlivening influence of his example; to the Venerable Deshung Rinpoche, profound Sakyapa scholar and compassionate spiritual friend, for his broad and precise replies to questions on doctrine, practice, lineage and texts; to Lama Tsengyur Rinpoche (Tsewong Gyurme), Kalu Rinpoche's chief representative in North America, for his patient attention to all my questions on colloquial and technical terms, and for providing the instructions for practice; to Tibetan scholar and translator Lobsang P. Lhalungpa, for generously sharing his expertise in language and philosophy, and for taking on the tedious but essential task of correcting my preliminary translation; and to the Venerable Chögyam Trungpa, Rinpoche, for the long and fruitful interview.

Above all, I am indebted to my friends Ingrid and Ken McLeod, translators and interpreters at Kagyu Kunkhyab Chuling, for tirelessly assisting me through four years of language difficulties, with no concern for recognition or reward; and to my husband Merv, for constant criticism and encouragement.

Judith Hanson

ABBREVIATIONS

The following abbreviations are used in the notes:

JAOS: *Journal of the American Oriental Society.*
JRAS: *Journal of the Royal Asiatic Society.*
Kosa: La Vallée Poussin, L. de. "L'Abhidharmakosa de Vasubandhu," *Mélanges Chinois et Bouddhiques*. Bruxelles: Institut Belge des Hautes Études Chinoises, 1971, vol. 16.
Lama: Lama Tsengyur Rinpoche (Tsewong Gyurme).
LPL: Lobsang P. Lhalungpa.
'Phags-lam: dBang-phyug rDorje, Karmapa IX, and others. *sGrub-brgyud Karma Kam-tshang-pa'i phyag-chen lhan-cig skyes-sbyor-gyi sngon-'gro bzhi-sbyor sogs-kyi ngag-'don 'phags-lam bgrod-pa'i shing-rta: Karma Kam-tshang sngon-'gro. gDams-ngag-mdzod*, vol. 6, fols. 105-22. Delhi: N. Lungtok and N. Gyaltsan, 1971. This contains the liturgy to be chanted during practice of the Four Foundations.
Skt.: Sanskrit.

Introduction

1: Description and Background

The Torch of Certainty is an annotated translation of the Tibetan Buddhist meditation manual *Nges-don sgron-me* by Jamgon Kongtrul ('Jammgon Kong-sprul blo-gros mtha'-yas-pa, 1813-99). It contains practical instructions and theoretical explanations of the "Four Foundations," (*sngon-'gro*) the most basic practices of the Kagyud sect of Tibetan Buddhism.

Nges-don sgron-me is a commentary on the brief "root" text *Lhan-cig skyes-sbyor khrid* by the ninth Karmapa, Wongchug Dorje (dBang-phyug rDorje, 1556-1603). According to Deshung Rinpoche, the latter is the shortest of three similar texts by the same author. The intermediate one is *Nges-don rgya-mtsho* and the longest is *Chos-sku mdzub-tshugs*.

The final section of *Nges-don sgron-me* contains instructions on the higher Mahamudra stage of doctrine and practice. This has not been translated.

Throughout the text, Kongtrul writes in a semicolloquial style, using irregular spelling, grammar and sentence structure not found in "classical" Tibetan works such as Gampopa's *Jewel Ornament of Liberation*.

According to Kalu Rinpoche, *Nges-don sgron-me* provides exoteric instructions (*thun-mong-gi gdams-ngag*) on meditation according to the Karma Kagyud sect of Mahayana-Vajrayana Buddhism.

Nges-don sgron-me is not read during actual meditation sessions, but is studied before and between sessions as needed. The ninth Karmapa's *'Phags-lam bgrod-pa'i shing-rta*,[1] the liturgy which is chanted aloud during these sessions, has not been included in this work.

Before we describe the actual meditations, a few remarks on the nature of a Tibetan Buddhist sect, on the Karma Kagyud sect and on Jamgon Kongtrul will be useful.

NATURE OF A TIBETAN BUDDHIST SECT

A sect within Tibetan Buddhism is identified by several factors. According to Tibetan teachers, the most important is the multidimensional phenomenon known as "lineage." The central lineage of a sect includes the succession of teachers—from the Buddha, through the Indian masters, up to contemporary Tibetans—who transmitted the oral and written teachings. Specialized lineages within a major sect include the teachers who transmitted instructions for the practices especially emphasized by that sect. These lineages will include some, but not all, of the teachers in the central lineage.

Another factor is the body of oral and written teachings produced by members of these lineages. This includes the *shung* (*zhung*), or authoritative Indian and Tibetan treatises, as well as other commentaries, instructional texts and ritual manuals.

A sect is also identified by its particular style of practice. The Kagyud sect, which places great emphasis on meditation, is commonly called a meditative tradition (*sgrub-brgyud*); while the Kadampa or Gelugpa sect is known as a tradition of intellectual discipline (*blo-sbyong-brgyud*).

Another identifying feature at one time was the group of monasteries in which the monks and nuns lived, studied and practiced. One monastery was usually the official headquarters for the sect and model for the others. Each of the four major sects had scores of monasteries, while some minor subsects seem to have had only one or two.

Lastly, a sect is identified by its spiritual head who is usually a high-ranking tulku.

THE KAGYUD SECT

Although Buddhism was known in Tibet as early as the sixth century A.D., the four major sects—the Nyingmapa, Sakyapa, Kadampa (later absorbed into the Gelugpa) and Kagyudpa did not emerge until the eleventh century.

The Kagyudpa lineage begins with the Buddha Vajradhara (Dorje Chang), symbol of supreme enlightenment. Vajradhara is not an historical Buddha like Shakyamuni, but one of many ever-present enlightened beings who continually dispense their blessings. Any individual involved in Kagyudpa practice is urged to view his guru as Vajradhara in order to bring the Buddha closer and ensure the fruitfulness of the guru-disciple relationship.

The second member of the lineage is the Indian *mahasiddha* Tilopa (988-1069). He is said to have received instruction directly from Vajradhara through visions and other extraordinary means.

The third member of the lineage is the Indian Naropa (1016-1100), Tilopa's long-suffering disciple.[2]

From Tilopa and Naropa originate the meditative practices with which the sect is identified: the Six Yogas of Naropa (*Na-ro'i chos-drug*) and Mahamudra (*Phyag-rgya-chen-po*).

The first two divisions of the sect originated with two Tibetan disciples of Naropa. Khyungpo the *yogin* (1002-64) founded the Shangpa Kagyud. Marpa the translator (1012-96) founded the Dagpo (Dwagspo) Kagyud. We will deal only with the latter.

Marpa was a layman whose thirst for learning drove him to undertake three costly and perilous journeys to India. Each time, he obtained important oral and written teachings. His momentous meeting with Naropa, which Tilopa had prophesied, inspired his career as a major proponent of the Vajrayana in Tibet.

Marpa transmitted Naropa's instructions to several disciples. The most famous was Milarepa (1052-1135).[3] To compensate for an early career in destructive black magic, Mila had to undergo years of painful and frustrating service to his seemingly cruel and irrational guru. Whenever Mila began to despair, Marpa would give some hopeful sign. Thus, Mila persisted for several years. After finally receiving the desired instructions, he spent his life meditating in solitude, composing his famous songs[4] and teaching.

Milarepa's best known disciple was Gampopa or Dagpo Lharje (1079-1153). He founded many monasteries including Dagpo, after which this division of the Kagyud sect is named. Gampopa became Mila's disciple only after a thorough training in the intellectual and moral discipline of the Kadampa system. Mila instructed him in the meditative techniques transmitted by Tilopa, Naropa and Marpa. Gampopa ". . . combined the teachings of the bKa'-gdams and the experiences of Mahamudra in a unique manner so that the two streams united."[5] Kagyud writers to the present day have drawn heavily on Gampopa's voluminous works.

Gampopa's disciples founded the subsects of the Dagpo Kagyudpa, the "Great Four" and the "Lesser Eight."

"Great Four"
(Founded by Gampopa's immediate disciples)

1. Karma Kagyud, founded by Dusum Khyenpa (1110-93).
2. Baram Kagyud, founded by Barampa Dharma Wongchug (ca. 1100).
3. Tshalpa Kagyud, founded by Tsondragpa (1123-94).
4. Phamo Kagyud, founded by Phamodrupa (1110-70).

"Lesser Eight"
(Founded by Phamodrupa's disciples)

1. Drikhung Kagyud.
2. Talung Kagyud.
3. Tropu Kagyud.
4. Drugpa Kagyud or Tod-drug, and its subsects:
5. May-drug.
6. Bar-drug.
7. Bar-ra.
8. Lho-drug.

From their inception in the twelfth and thirteenth centuries until the Chinese takeover in 1959, these subsects have been active throughout Tibet. Some, most notably the Karma and Drugpa Kagyud, now have monasteries in India, Nepal, Bhutan, Sikkim and Scotland. Most of the Tibetan Buddhist centers which have appeared in Europe and North America in the past ten years were founded by two Karma Kagyud Lamas: Chögyam Trungpa, Rinpoche and Kalu Rinpoche.[6]

THE KARMA KAGYUD SECT

The Karma Kagyud sect was founded by Dusum Khyenpa (1110-93), the first Karmapa. The Karmapa is its highest tulku, and spiritual head. According to Kalu Rinpoche, the Karmapa is the supreme spiritual authority for all the Kagyud subsects. As such, he officiates at key rituals and is responsible for recognition of all the important Kagyudpa tulkus.

Karma Kagyudpas consider his spiritual status to be equal to that of the Dalai Lama, head of the Gelugpa sect. Both are considered incarnations of Avalokiteshvara, Bodhisattva of compassion. Both are addressed as "wish-fulfilling gem" (*yid-bzhin nor-bu*). But unlike the Dalai Lama, the Karmapa was not officially connected with the central government; i.e., he is not considered an incarnation of Songtsen Gampo or another Tibetan ruler and has never shared the Dalai Lama's role as a national symbol.

Although the Karmapa's official seat was at Tshurpu monastery in central Tibet, most of the Karmapas were born in Kham (eastern Tibet). Presently, the Karmapa's official seat is at Rumtek monastery in Sikkim.

The Karmapas exercised great spiritual and political influence in Kham. Many of them maintained diplomatic ties with China and enjoyed Imperial patronage.[7]

The Karmapa is referred to as "Wearer of the Black Hat." This hat, like a mitre, is a symbol of his spiritual authority. The original black hat is said to have been presented to Dusum Khyenpa by the dakinis, who wove it from the hair of a hundred thousand of their kind. According to Kalu Rinpoche, this original hat was invisible to all but those of great merit. A material replica was given to the fifth Karmapa Deshin Shegpa (1384-1415) by the Yung-lo Emperor Ch'êng-tsu so that the black hat, a mere glimpse of which is said to guarantee the beholder's rebirth in the higher realms, might be seen by all.[8]

This replica is thought to be the same one donned by the present Karmapa, His Holiness Rongjung rigpay Dorje (b. 1924), when he performed the Black Hat Ceremony in Europe and North America in 1974. This ceremony is the key ritual of the Karmapas. It re-enacts the original "coronation" of Dusum Khyenpa by the dakinis, reaffirming the place of each Karmapa in the Karmapa line and invoking Avalokiteshvara as the source of that lineage.

There have been sixteen Karmapas to date:

1. Dusum Khyenpa (1110-93).
2. Karma Pakshi (1206-83).
3. Rongjung Dorje (1284-1339).
4. Rolpay Dorje (1340-83).
5. Deshin Shegpa (1384-1415).
6. Tongwa Dondan (1416-53).
7. Chodrag Gyatso (1454-1506).
8. Michod Dorje (1507-54).
9. Wongchug Dorje (1556-1603).
10. Choying Dorje (1604-74).
11. Yeshe Dorje (1675-1702).
12. Jongchub Dorje (1703-32).
13. Dudul Dorje (1733-97).
14. Tegchog Dorje (1797-ca. 1845).
15. Khakhyab Dorje (ca. 1845-1924).
16. Rongjung rigpay Dorje (b. 1924).[9]

This list includes several statesmen, authors, and teachers.

The present Karmapa was educated at Tshurpu and now lives at Rumtek monastery in Sikkim, the new seat of the Karma Kagyudpa.

Other important tulkus of the sect include the Shamar (Zhva-dmar) or "Red Hat" Rinpoche, and the Situ, Gyaltshab and Pawo Rinpoches. The Shamar line enjoyed periods of political power in central Tibet but was officially terminated in the late eighteenth century due to the ninth tulku's complicity in a Nepalese invasion. The line was revived by the present Karmapa. The new Shamarpa was born in the early 1950's and lives at Rumtek.

All the Karmapas and most of the key tulkus of the sect are members of the "Golden Rosary of Wish-Fulfilling Gems," the specialized Karma Kagyud lineage of Mahamudra teachers. A few others are included in this Mahamudra lineage because they were teachers or prominent disciples of a Karmapa. One of these few is our author Jamgon Kongtrul, tutor to the fifteenth Karmapa.

BIOGRAPHICAL SKETCH OF JAMGON KONGTRUL

Jamgon Kongtrul (1813-99) was a versatile and prolific scholar whose works span the entire field of traditional Tibetan learning. Characterized by Smith[10] as a "Tibetan Leonardo," Kongtrul was also a respected physician, diplomat and powerful politician in his native Kham (eastern Tibet).

Before receiving any Buddhist training, Kongtrul was thoroughly schooled in Bon by his nominal father Sonam Pel, a Bon Lama. Kongtrul himself believed his natural father to be the Buddhist Lama Yungdrung Tendzin of the eminent Khyungpo lineage.

Kongtrul's earliest Buddhist training was in the Nyingma tradition, into which he was ordained at Zhe-chen monastery in 1832. A year later, however, to qualify for a literary post at Palpung monastery, he had to take reordination as a Karma Kagyud monk, a requirement whose "... pettiness and sectarianism distressed Kongtrul. . . ."[11]

This second ordination was conferred by Situ Padma Nyinjay (1774-1853) whom Kongtrul invokes in *Nges-don sgron-me* as his "root-guru." He was then given the name with which he signed this text, Ngawong Yontan Gyatso.

By thirty years of age Kongtrul had received teachings and empowerments from sixty Lamas of diverse sects and lineages. Around this time he was recognized as a tulku, a move whose intent was at least partly political.[12]

Kongtrul accepted the authenticity of *terma*[13] as did the Bonpos and Nyingmapas. In 1855 he was recognized as a *terton* by the terton Chogyur Lingpa (1829-79).

Together with the Khampa scholar Jamyang Khyentse Wongpo (1820-92), he initiated the "unbiased" or *rimay* (*ris-med*) movement, whose precursors date back to the fourteenth century. This religious and cultural renaissance emerged at least partly in reaction to the deadening influence of the closed sectarianism which had existed in Tibet for centuries. Its adherents did not give up their own sect-identity or focus but viewed the Lamas and teachings of all sects as equally worthy and freely pursued a varied curriculum of study and practice. The rimay movement attracted a number of outstanding scholars whose writings comprise the authoritative texts used by many modern Tibetan teachers, especially those of the Nyingma and Kagyud traditions.

During the many incidents of religio-political warfare in Kham, Kongtrul acted as a mediator, and later became a major political leader. Despite this chaotic atmosphere, he wrote more than ninety volumes on theory and practice according to the Nyingmapa, Kadampa, Sakyapa, Shijaypa and Bonpo, as well as the many branches of the Kagyud sect. In some works, designated as Rimaypa, he treats the topic from the viewpoint of each sect in turn.

Most of his writings are in the collection entitled *The Five Treasuries* (*mDzod-lnga*), printed at Palpung in the late nineteenth century. The present work, *Nges-don sgron-me* (1844), was one of his earliest.

NOTES

1. *sGrub-brgyud Karma Kam-tshang-pa'i phyag-chen lhan-cig skyes-sbyor-gyi sngon-'gro bzhi-sbyor sogs-kyi ngag-'don 'phags-lam bgrod-pa'i shing-rta: Karma Kam-tshang sngon-'gro. gDams-ngag-mdzod*, vol. 6, fols. 105-22. Delhi: N. Lungtok and N. Gyaltsan, 1971. Henceforth abbreviated as *'Phags-lam*.
2. See H. V. Guenther's *Life and Teaching of Naropa*. New York: Oxford, 1963, pp. 1–109.
3. See W. Y. Evans-Wentz, *Tibet's Great Yogi Milarepa*. New York: Oxford, 1957.
4. See G. C. C. Chang, *The Hundred Thousand Songs of Milarepa*. New York: University Books, 1962.
5. See H. V. Guenther's *Jewel Ornament of Liberation by sGam-po-pa*. Berkeley: Shambhala, 1971, pp. ix–x.
6. Kalu Rinpoche is also a member of the Shangpa Kagyud; in fact, he is the only surviving possessor of its complete transmission.
7. See H. E. Richardson, "The Karma-pa Sect," *JRAS*, 1958: 139–64; 1959: 1–18.
8. Related by Kalu Rinpoche at a public lecture in Vancouver, October 11, 1974, shortly before His Holiness' performance of the Black Hat Ceremony.

9. Adapted from Richardson, "The Karma-pa Sect," *JRAS*, 1959: 18.

10. Most of the material in this section is drawn from the single relevant source available in a Western language: Gene Smith's "Introduction" to Lokesh Chandra's edition of Kongtrul's *Ses-bya kun-khyab*. Satapitaka series, vol. 80. Delhi: Internat'l Acad. of Indian Culture, pp. 1–87.

11. Smith, "Introduction," p. 30.

12. Ibid., p. 31.

13. *gter-ma*: Texts and teachings which express Buddhist doctrine in contemporary terms. They are traditionally said to have been composed by Padmasambhava when he brought Buddhism to Tibet, and hidden by him until they would be needed. When required, they are rediscovered and promulgated by special teachers called *gter-ston*.

2: Practice of the Four Foundations

Before beginning a meditation session, the practitioner excludes all distractions. He may then set up an icon of the visualization used in that practice, e.g., an image of Vajrasattva, a picture of the Refuge tree, etc.

Actual practice of the Four Special Foundations involves the practitioner in an intense drama combining physical, verbal and mental acts. As he chants each section of the liturgy, he visualizes the scene described in it, considers the significance of the prayers and performs the ritual acts indicated. During all of this, he tries to focus his attention exclusively on the ritual.

To complete the practice, he must perform each of the Four Special Foundations 111,111 times. Since Taking Refuge also includes 111,111 full prostrations, the total is 555,555. Hence, the practice is commonly called the "Five-hundred-thousand."

The following interviews with three leading teachers of Tibetan Buddhism focus on the practice of the Four Foundations and its significance for modern students of Buddhism.

INTERVIEWS WITH KALU RINPOCHE, DESHUNG RINPOCHE AND CHÖGYAM TRUNGPA, RINPOCHE[1]

What are the Four Special Foundations and how do they fit into the whole scheme of Buddhist practice?

CHÖGYAM TRUNGPA, RINPOCHE: Every type of spiritual discipline, craft or educational system has its beginning, middle and concluding levels. The Four Foundations (*sngon-'gro*, literally "prelude") are the beginning of the Vajrayana discipline. Of course, the Vajrayana is not the first but the third level of Buddhist practice, to be preceded by the Hinayana and Mahayana. But those who begin the Vajrayana discipline do so with the Four Foundations.

According to tradition, the Foundation practices require a lot of preparation. In the early days in Tibet, people had to have a great deal of training before practicing the Foundations. This included basic training in tranquility and insight meditation (*zhi-gnas* and *lhag-mthong;* Skt.

shamatha and *vipashyana*), as well as some training in the Mahayana,
which included formally receiving the Bodhisattva vow, and so on.

What is the function of each of the Four Special Foundations?

KALU RINPOCHE: Generally speaking, the first 444,444 practices (i.e.,
Refuge and prostrations, Vajrasattva, and the Mandala-Offering) clear
away obscurations (see chap. 3, n. 12 and chap. 5, n. 24) and gather the
Two Accumulations (see chap. 1, n. 20). The Guru-Yoga gives you
great faith in your guru which leads to your receipt of his blessing and
attainment of Mahamudra.

TRUNGPA, RINPOCHE: The Four Special Foundations are an evolutionary
process in which each event has a definite place. They could be connected
with the Four Dharmas of Gampopa. In Taking Refuge, your mind begins to follow the Dharma, which is the First Dharma of Gampopa. Your
attitude toward yourself and toward everything in your life becomes
connected purely with Dharma practice. There is no longer such a thing
as a division between sacred and profane.

To begin to practice, you must first "give in" to the Dharma completely. This is accomplished by doing prostrations, a process of complete
surrender, of definite commitment. I don't think anyone can begin
Vajrayana practice without that.

When you take the Bodhisattva vow, having decided to go and
having bought your ticket, you actually begin the journey—*bodhicitta*
and the Bodhisattva path. This is related to the Second Dharma of
Gampopa, which is that your Dharma practice can actually win success
on the path.

When you do the Vajrasattva practice, having already surrendered,
you have to purify and further acknowledge what you have surrendered.
All the impurities must be purified.

After purification, something still remains—the pure person, which
might contain some stain of arrogance, some stain of existence. In the
Mandala practice you actually give everything, including the pure person. You offer this—the giver—as well as all the offerings, at which
point, in a sense, you no longer exist.

By the time you reach the Guru-Yoga practice, you are psycho-
logically ready to identify with your guru, and immense devotion is born
in your mind. This is connected with the Third Dharma of Gampopa,
which is that, in following the path, confusion could be clarified. The
actual transformation of confusion into wisdom, the Fourth Dharma of

Gampopa, is receiving abhishekas and practicing various sadhanas. This is the main part of the Vajrayana discipline, which comes much later.

Were the Four Foundations practiced by sects other than the Kagyudpa? If so, how did their ways of practicing differ?

KALU RINPOCHE: Yes, the Four Foundations were practiced by all Tibetan sects. They were practiced in basically the same way by all the sects, with certain substitutions which reflected the interests of each sect. For example, the lineage of gurus visualized in the practices would vary from sect to sect.

In Taking Refuge, the Sakyapas, like the Kagyudpas, would use Vajradhara as the central figure; the Nyingmapas would use Padmasambhava, and the Gelugpas would use Buddha Shakyamuni.

Also in Taking Refuge, the yidams and dharmapalas would vary from sect to sect. For example, Vajrabhairava would be the chief Gelugpa dharmapala instead of the Kagyudpa's Mahakala (Bernagche).

In the meditation on Vajrasattva, some sects would use the *yab-yum* form of Vajrasattva instead of the one we use. Even some Kagyudpas would use this form.

As for the Mandala-Offering, the visualization is the same for all sects, but the liturgy varies somewhat from sect to sect.

The Guru-Yoga practice is virtually the same for all sects, but the liturgies differ slightly.

DESHUNG RINPOCHE: My own tradition, the Sakyapa, practices the Four Foundations in a manner very similar to that of the Kagyudpa. One difference, however, lies in the vow of refuge. We use the fourfold vow instead of the sixfold one used by the Kagyudpas, that is, "We take refuge in the Guru; we take refuge in the Buddha; we take refuge in the Dharma; we take refuge in the Sangha." In addition, we visualize Vajrasattva in *yab-yum*. We usually use the mandala of seven features instead of the one with thirty-seven features used by the Kagyudpa.

The Gelugpas added three "hundred-thousand" practices to the "Five-hundred-thousand" practiced by other sects. Their additions consist of 111,111 *tsa-tsa*, water and flower offerings. Thus, their practice of the Foundations is called the "Eight-hundred-thousand."

Do these other sects use the Four Special Foundations as a main practice, as does the Kagyudpa?

KALU RINPOCHE: Yes, with minor differences in emphasis between sects.

DESHUNG RINPOCHE: In the Sakya sect, there was generally more leeway allowed as to the amount of emphasis an individual would place on the Four Foundations. In many instances, a person would practice Taking Refuge for three days before practicing a meditation on the yidam Hevajra. Sometimes a person would practice the Vajrasattva meditation for three days in preparation for Hevajra meditation.

It is important to realize, however, that in Tibet comparatively few monks of any sect had either the leisure or the inclination to practice a great deal of meditation of any kind, the Four Foundations included. For example, in Kalu Rinpoche's monastery of Palpung, of the five or six hundred monks who lived there, only seventy or so would have been practicing the Four Foundations intensively at any one time. The others were preoccupied with their monastic duties, memorization of texts and participation in numerous group empowerment rituals.

In what ways, if any, will the manner of practicing the Four Foundations here in the West differ from that followed in Tibet? Will Westerners find the Foundations easier or more difficult to practice?

KALU RINPOCHE: The way of practicing the Foundations will be basically the same here as it was in Tibet. In Tibet there were people; here there are people. In Tibet they had defilements; here they have defilements. However, Westerners do seem to have the additional problem of doubt, of unwillingness to accept the validity of the teachings. This stems from your superior education in worldly matters. On the positive side, Westerners can learn the Dharma very quickly as compared to the length of time it took Tibetans to learn it.

DESHUNG RINPOCHE: The Foundations will certainly be practiced the same way here as in Tibet. After all, Tibetans and Westerners can both be Buddhists. Because of the good karma Westerners have accumulated, the interest and opportunity to practice the Foundations is much greater here than it was in Tibet. Westerners have the additional advantage of not having broken their sacred commitments (*dam-tshig,* see chap. 1, n. 10) since they thus far have very few commitments to break! This is a factor which will promote the effectiveness of the practice.

TRUNGPA, RINPOCHE: Because of the cultural differences, the practice of the Four Foundations will be somewhat different for Western students. Since they are not completely familiar with the cultural background of Buddhism, when they try to practice the Foundations they will encounter some cultural gaps which they will have to overcome. We must try not to impose the Tibetan tradition on them but to present them with the basic "mind's work" of the teachings.

One problem in the West is that people are accustomed to focusing on their bodies. The whole society is based on comfort. Western students practicing the Foundations make a big issue of their aches and pains, and tend to get very attached and exaggerate them.

An important difference is that Western students need a lot more prior training in the Hinayana and Mahayana so that they will know what they are doing when they practice the Foundations. Since they lack the cultural background of Tibetans, when introduced to the Foundations they will not be ready to jump into the practices immediately, and they may see them as alien, as some sort of a gimmick. We cannot respond to their doubts by telling them to shut up and have faith. To help them overcome these doubts, we must train them in tranquility and insight meditation much more thoroughly than was done in Tibet. Apart from these, I don't see any particular differences.

Before an individual practices the Four Special Foundations, what should he study and/or practice first?

KALU RINPOCHE: Before a person begins to practice the Four Foundations, he should formally take the vow of refuge from a guru in addition to taking some other Vajrayana empowerment. The Vajrasattva empowerment is recommended before practicing that meditation.

Before he can practice the Four Special Foundations, an individual must study the "four thoughts which turn the mind toward religion" (see chap. 1). He must also learn as much as possible about the meaning of the Foundations and must be instructed in their practice by a guru.

DESHUNG RINPOCHE: Before practicing the Four Special Foundations, a person must apply the "four thoughts which turn the mind toward religion." If he thinks these over carefully and learns to appreciate their meaning, his practice will be very effective and fruitful; otherwise, it will be sheer gibberish. In short, as the Buddha said: "Abandon all unwholesome action. Perform as much wholesome action as you can. Learn to control your own mind—this is Buddha's teaching." A person who is setting out to discipline and control his mind must first understand the significance of the precious human existence, impermanence and so on. These will constitute a solid basis for practice.

TRUNGPA, RINPOCHE: As I have said, before he tries to practice the Foundations, an individual must be thoroughly trained in tranquility and insight meditation. In addition, he must be familiar with the basic teachings of Buddhism, such as the Four Noble Truths, Six Perfections and five skandhas, so that when he is introduced to the Vajrayana via the Four Foundations it will not seem like a foreign product.

What type of person should practice the Four Foundations?

KALU RINPOCHE: It does not matter if the person is a monk, layman, educated, uneducated, male, female and so on. A person who wishes to practice the Foundations need only possess the following qualities: he should feel disgusted with samsara and be acutely aware of its inherent misery; he should appreciate the qualities of fully enlightened existence, perfect Buddhahood.

   In addition, persons who find it difficult to generate compassion and to understand emptiness should practice the Four Foundations. This is because lack of compassion and difficulty in understanding emptiness reveal that the individual has many obscurations. The best way to remove these is to practice the Four Special Foundations.

DESHUNG RINPOCHE: The most important prerequisites for practicing the Four Foundations are faith and confidence. As it is said, "All dharmas arise in interdependence." This especially applies to phenomena like faith and conviction. If a person who has no faith tries to practice Dharma, it is as if he were planting a burnt seed. A person who has no faith is unlikely to be interested in practicing the Foundations in the first place. Even if he does practice them, they will not do him much good.

   If a person has faith, all other factors, such as age, sex, monastic or lay status, and so on, become unimportant. But generally speaking, it is best if the Foundations are practiced by an ordained monk or nun, or a layman who has taken the five precepts (and become an *upasaka*). But even a householder becomes an *upasaka* by receiving any Vajrayana empowerment.

TRUNGPA, RINPOCHE: It doesn't matter. Any type of person can do these practices. As long as an individual has become involved in tranquility and insight meditation, his personality has begun to dissolve somewhat. By the time he gets involved in the Vajrayana through the Foundations, he is no longer a "type of person," particularly—he is already there!

What role does the guru play in guiding an individual through practice

of the Foundations before, during and after completion of the practices?
What is the nature of the guru-disciple relationship?

KALU RINPOCHE: Before he begins to practice the Foundations, an individual needs a guru to give him the instructions for practice.

During the course of the practice, if he understands it well, he will not need a guru's guidance. If he encounters serious obstacles, he should rely on the guru's advice. If minor obstacles arise, he should try to deal with them himself by realizing that they are simply the outcome of his own former actions. If he becomes seriously ill, he should not be discouraged but should cease practicing and joyfully anticipate his future resumption of the practice.

After he has completed the Four Foundations, the individual must rely on the guru for further teachings, including instructions in yidam meditations and so on.

DESHUNG RINPOCHE: Regarding the role of the guru, it is said: "All the wonderful qualities which arise in a disciple stem from his spiritual friend (the guru)."

Before practicing the Foundations, the individual needs a guru to instruct him in the practices.

While he is practicing, he should continue to rely on the guru for further explanation of the meaning and benefits of each practice.

After he completes the Foundations, the individual needs the guru to instruct him in Mahamudra practices, for which the Four Foundations have prepared him.

Until you attain enlightenment, your entire religious career depends on the guru. The fact that all the great Bodhisattvas have their guru seated on the crown on their heads—for example, Amitabha on Avalokiteshvara's head and so on—shows that even Bodhisattvas still rely on their gurus. Your guru embodies your sacred commitment to keep enlightenment foremost in your mind until you actually achieve it.

TRUNGPA, RINPOCHE: A person who is practicing the Vajrayana discipline should have some notion of what is known as the "vajra master" or root-guru who instructs us in the Vajrayana. In each of the three yanas the teacher has a different role. In the Hinayana he is the elder (Skt. *sthavira*), or wise man. In the Mahayana he is the good spiritual friend (Skt. *kalyanamitra*). In the Vajrayana he is the master—almost a dictator—who tells us what to do. The relationship must be very strong, definite and direct—one of great devotion.

When you practice the Foundations, your prostrations are directed toward your root-guru as Vajradhara in person. If your relationship with your guru is not very strong, this practice will be very feeble.

In these practices, Vajradhara has two aspects. The first, the Dharmakaya or primordial aspect of Buddha—the awakened state of mind or the general existence of full enlightenment without any obstacles, obscurities or definitions—is the Vajradhara at the head of the lineage [i.e., the top of the refuge tree]. The second aspect of Vajradhara is that very concept, transplanted into your personal root-guru. So your root-guru is the Buddha in person, not only in the sense of a Nirmanakaya like Gautama Buddha, but Vajradhara himself—the complete Buddha. So the reference to Vajradhara is tied up with the notion of trust and faith in your root-guru.

It has been said that the guru's body is the Sangha, his speech is the Dharma, and his mind is the Buddha. In this case, Buddha has three aspects: Nirmanakaya, Sambhogakaya and Dharmakaya. So the guru-Buddha includes the whole thing.

Of great importance in the guru-disciple relationship is the samaya-bond (*dam-tshig*), the commitment established between you and your guru once you have undertaken the Vajrayana discipline. Although you may not yet have received any empowerments from him, once you have taken him on as your Vajrayana teacher the commitment has already been made and the bond established absolutely. There is no such thing as a mediocre samaya-bond.

Commitment to your guru and his teachings is very necessary; it gives you some guidelines for your life. Without that commitment you might begin to make up your own version of the Dharma, your own edition of the teachings, and sooner or later what you will get back is just your own ego version of the teachings. So the idea of commitment here is total surrendering, complete surrendering. You don't edit your own version of the Dharma anymore.

The commitment allows you to receive the pure teachings undiluted by the influence of ego. Commitment keeps the teachings clean, pure and workable, so that the actual teaching, the teaching in its pure form, works for you. Maybe the teacher might be pure, and the teachings might be pure, but if you don't commit yourself properly, then you end up putting a part of yourself into the teachings, and you don't receive the pure thing. It's like drinking out of a dirty cup.

If a student tries to practice the Foundations without a guru's guidance, probably nothing will happen, except that his confusion will increase. It will be a waste of time.

What is the importance of the Mahamudra lineage for one who is practicing the Foundations?

TRUNGPA, RINPOCHE: The lineage is very important for the practitioner. Each teacher in the lineage had his particular skillful way of teaching. Each has contributed a great deal to the wealth of the Kagyud tradition. Each one's life is a perfect example for us to study. Each one has left behind and passed on his experiences to us.

The lineage shows us that "it can be done"—even by us! It makes us aware that the teachings represent not one but many lifetimes of work. Each teacher sacrificed a lot, went through a great deal of personal hardship and finally attained enlightenment. Belonging to this lineage makes us very rich and full of enlightenment-wealth. Being part of this family gives us immense encouragement and also a sense of validity [regarding that which we are trying to practice]. We realize that the teachings we now receive have come down from all of them.

The lineage also enables us to place ourselves within a certain geography. We have happened upon somebody who has opened up the whole thing for us—like a gigantic rain descending on us!

What is the significance of the physical, verbal and mental techniques used in practice of the Four Foundations?

TRUNGPA, RINPOCHE: Prostrations originally came from the Indian tradition where you make a gesture of reverence to somebody higher than you. The idea of prostrations is that you have found somebody who is utterly worthy for you to open to, completely. So you fall on the ground and touch your forehead at his feet. Then you find something more to do, which is called nine-fold prostrations, where nine joints of your body are completely on the ground. That's the final idea of prostrations, which is much more elaborate and definite; physically you are really doing something.

In the Mandala practice you are offering your wealth and yourself at the same time. You feel happy that you can walk on earth, you feel that the earth is yours, in some sense, and you just give all that in the form of piles of rice.

Mt. Meru, the four continents, etc., which are represented by the piles of rice, comprise the traditional universe derived from Hindu mythology. This is strictly a cultural phenomenon: in those days the universe consisted of that. In modern times we might offer the solar system, and so on. The basic idea is that you are giving the world you live in and also the symbols of work, sense-perceptions, basically everything that is worthwhile.

The geography is meant to be discussed. I hope that some day a conference will be called by Buddhist leaders in which we can discuss the geographical aspects and come up with some solution.

When we chant the liturgy in all the Foundation practices, we actually say it. In ordinary life when we are very involved with ourselves, we usually talk to ourselves. In this case you actually *say* it, which makes it much steadier and more solid—something definite happens.

The mantras we chant in these practices are not regarded as the same as the mantras used in the more advanced sadhana practices. Here, it's still just a process rather than the actual, real mantras in higher forms of Vajrayana. For example, the Vajrasattva mantra, which is a purification mantra, has 100 syllables which contain the bijas for one hundred peaceful and wrathful deities. These are said in a certain way which invokes the essence which would be fundamentally, inherently pure. But it's still a superficial use of mantra here, in some sense.

Visualization, the mental technique used in all Four Foundations, is something that most people find very difficult to do. In Vajrayana, visualization is called Kye-rim, or the Developing Stage of meditation. It is slightly different from how we normally think of visualizing. Ordinarily, we think of visualization as just day dreaming. In this case, it is taking the complete attitude of the deity, mentally actually seeing it, rather than purely day dreaming it. This requires prior training—basically, sitting practice, which is tranquility and insight meditation. Even people who have undergone this training have a lot of difficulty with visualization. But you have to start with the teaching of Nirmanakaya, rather than relating first to Dharmakaya. You have to start with body and then work with mind. Otherwise it will be very difficult.

Traditionally, while students are going through the Four Foundation practices, they are also taught certain particular formless meditations which are connected more closely to the Mahamudra principle. That is the notion of the Fulfillment Stage or Dzog-rim, which is always recommended a great deal. There should always be the Developing Stage and the Fulfillment Stage together, visualization and formless meditation together. Without that, somehow the whole thing is like fingerpainting rather than actually doing it. There are different levels of formless, of course. Students usually begin by borrowing the Hinayana practice of tranquility and insight meditation, and then out of that some glimpse of the Mahamudra experience might occur. That seems to be very important. The idea is not to trust purely in the gadgets of the practices alone, but that there is something happening behind that. Some kind of unseen, unformed—I don't know what you'd call it. The incomprehensible is comprehended, with just a few glimpses. That has to happen. Traditionally that is done, and I did that myself.

Dzog-rim or the Fulfillment Stage is a general term. There are different levels of Dzog-rim or formless meditation. From the Hinayanist point of view, it would be shamatha and vipashyana, tranquility and insight meditation. From the Mahayanist's point of view, it would be Maitri bhavana or something like that. From Vajrayana, Dzog-rim is finally Mahamudra. But you can't have that just suddenly given to you without previous training. That's why the basic training in shamatha and vipashyana is very important.

This idea of Dzog-rim or formless meditation is traditionally handed down from teacher to student. It's not talked about even in the commentaries. That's the company policy, so to speak. That is true for this text, *The Torch of Certainty*, as well. This commentary is very basic, direct and written with a lot of heart, a lot of soul. It's nice that people can read it. At the same time, I feel that people shouldn't just pick up the book and try to practice without a teacher. We have to take some kind of measures to protect the teachings, so that they can be presented properly. I feel some concern about this, and I think the dharmapalas will be behind my shoulders, trying to mind my business: they always are.

In what surroundings should the Four Foundations be practiced?

KALU RINPOCHE: The ideal environment for practice is one of complete isolation. Lack of external stimuli facilitates practice. If this is not feasible, it is fine to live with others, to engage in other activities, see friends, and so on. In that case, one should try to practice at least one to four hours a day, during which time one should not speak to others or interact with them in any way.

DESHUNG RINPOCHE: In the Buddhist tradition, disengagement from worldly activities during religious practice is very highly regarded. In solitude, one can devote all one's energies to practice. It is said: "Through disengagement of the body and speech from worldly activities comes disengagement of the mind." This is the best way to practice—in an isolated retreat. But even practicing in the home, where there may be many distractions, is indeed wonderful.

TRUNGPA, RINPOCHE: People have a problem deciding whether to practice in a group or alone. Generally, Vajrayana practice should be done in groups. In the Vajrayana there is much more idea of sangha than in the Hinayana or the spiritual brotherhood of the Mahayana. In Vajrayana the concept of the vajra sangha is very important and very necessary. Actually, people might practice the Four Foundations in groups together or by themselves. It doesn't make that much difference. The main point is that you can't expect ideal surroundings; there would be no such thing, particularly, as ideal surroundings. People can't afford to take a whole year off from work, and they have their families and so on. Of course, in Tibet in the monasteries we had retreat centers, and we practiced quite a lot together. [To work with this situation here] I have some of my students practice the Foundations in groups. We have set up prostration shrine rooms, Vajrasattva mantra shrine rooms, and mandala shrine rooms. The basic principle of practicing together is what's known as the vajra feast: once you join the Vajrayana discipline there should be no holding back of yourself; everything should be shared together. It's also a question of transmitting the insight that comes out of group practice, sharing that with your brothers and sisters in the Dharma, rather than keeping it secret. It doesn't particularly have to be a group-encounter type of situation, but just feeling, and being together. When people achieve an understanding of the Fulfillment Stage of meditation, or Mahamudra, there are some psychological happenings that can actually be felt as well as said by the whole group. Everybody's prostrating together; you are in the same boat. The idea is that it should be more normal, definitely, rather than that you are doing some funny thing while your wife or husband, and your kids are away.

Must the Four Foundations always be practiced in the order in which they are presented in The Torch of Certainty?

KALU RINPOCHE: This order is certainly the best, but if circumstances prohibit practice of the Foundations in this order, or if one wishes to combine two of the Foundations to avoid becoming overtired from doing so many prostrations at once, or if one works at a very demanding job and cannot do prostrations, one may begin with the meditation of Vajrasattva and the Mandala-Offering. One may even begin with the Guru-Yoga.

TRUNGPA, RINPOCHE: The order should be kept the same. Each stage prepares for the next, and they become increasingly more subtle until you reach Guru-Yoga, which is complete devotion to the Guru. Having evolved to this level, you are prepared to receive abhishekas.

If an individual can only practice one of the Foundations in his lifetime, which one should he practice?

KALU RINPOCHE: He should follow his own inclinations.

If an individual loses interest in the practice, should he stop and wait for the inspiration to return, or keep practicing?

KALU RINPOCHE: He should definitely keep practicing. If he finds that his thoughts wander a great deal, he should end the session and simply try to let his mind rest, but he should resume the practice as soon as possible.

TRUNGPA, RINPOCHE: Losing interest in the practice is a symptom of not having enough training in tranquility and insight meditation. Training in tranquility and insight makes you, first of all, very aware of your pain and your neuroses. It increases your mindfulness and enables you to begin to make friends with yourself. You learn how to be by yourself, with yourself. Without this training, you might easily become overwhelmed and put off by the physical exertion and mechanical aspect of these practices.

If a person finds himself put off and feels that he cannot continue the Foundations, he should return to tranquility and insight meditation and go back to the Vajrayana discipline later on.

What type of practice schedule is best?

KALU RINPOCHE: This is entirely up to the individual. If he has no other occupation, four sessions a day, each lasting at least an hour, is ideal. If he does have other work to do, he should attempt one session in the morning and one in the evening. But there is no compulsory schedule.

How much time is required to complete the Four Foundations?

KALU RINPOCHE: This, of course, depends on the individual's schedule. Refuge and prostrations usually take quite a long time to complete, as does the Vajrasattva meditation. The Mandala-Offering and the Guru-Yoga take less time.

How many times should an individual practice the Four Foundations—once in his life, or more often?

KALU RINPOCHE: If he can do it once, this is very wonderful. If he then feels very positive about this method of clearing away obscurations and wants to repeat the practices, this is also very wonderful and will have the same effect as his first attempt.

DESHUNG RINPOCHE: My root-guru, Ngawong Lepa, performed the 111,111 prostrations forty times during his life, and some of the other practices a similar number of times. This was comparatively rare. I have tried to follow his example and have done each practice several hundred-thousand times. But most people I knew in Tibet merely practiced Taking Refuge and so on for three days in preparation for yidam meditations.

What are the indications of successful practice?

KALU RINPOCHE: Increased faith, devotion, insight and compassion; a stronger interest in Dharma practice and lack of interest in worldly matters.

DESHUNG RINPOCHE: Increased faith, confidence and trust in your guru, and growing understanding of the workings of actions and results and so on are indications that your meditative practice has been effective and that meditation is becoming your way of life.

TRUNGPA, RINPOCHE: Basically, you will be less arrogant and less opinionated.

How does an individual know when his practice of the Four Foundations has been unsuccessful?

KALU RINPOCHE: The effects of unsuccessful practice will be the opposite of those of successful practice: the obscurations will increase, faith will diminish and so on.

DESHUNG RINPOCHE: (Uproarious laughter).[2] Lack of progress in these and other meditative practices manifests itself in the individual's attitudes. If he becomes increasingly concerned with worldly matters; if he develops greater and greater doubts about the qualities of the Three Jewels and denies the validity of the teachings; if he is less and less concerned about the welfare of others and has less and less confidence in his guru: this indicates lack of progress in meditation and receipt of the "blessing of Mara."

TRUNGPA, RINPOCHE: If you become more arrogant and opinionated, it means that you do not have enough compassion and sympathy and that something is wrong with your practice.

What should a person do if he feels that his practice has been unsuccessful?

KALU RINPOCHE: Failure of the practice is usually due to the person's inability to prevent his thoughts from wandering during practice and his being burdened with great obscurations. To correct this, he should ponder the "four thoughts" again. If so inclined, he should repeat the Foundation practices or rely on a yidam meditation such as that of Avalokiteshvara, which seems to be very effective in such situations.

DESHUNG RINPOCHE: An individual who has not made any progress should again practice Taking Refuge and do prostrations, and practice the Vajrasattva meditation to clear away the obscurations responsible for his lack of progress. He should practice the Guru-Yoga to increase his faith in the guru.

An individual's lack of progress is often due to the fact that he has not really begun to appreciate the precious human existence, impermanence and so on. If he appreciates these, true meditation will occur. Lack of this appreciation and lack of faith will obstruct true meditation.

TRUNGPA, RINPOCHE: If an individual's practice is not working, this is because he approaches it as some kind of gymnastics, due to a lack of genuine renunciation. He is still blinded by the confused world. In order to begin to see clearly, the practitioner should return to tranquility and insight meditation. This advice is not in conflict with that of the other Rinpoches. The "four thoughts" are a contemplative discipline by which you develop disgust with samsara. If you practice tranquility and insight as the basis of the whole spiritual journey, then the "four thoughts" will arise as a natural process.

For which further practices does completion of the Foundations prepare us?

KALU RINPOCHE: Since we are in the Vajrayana, completion of the Foundations enables us to practice all other Vajrayana meditations.

DESHUNG RINPOCHE: Completion of the Four Foundations enables us to practice all the major yidam meditations. In the Kagyud tradition this would include those of Cakrasamvara and Vajravarahi; in the Sakya tradition, Hevajra and Vajrayogini; in the Nyingma tradition, the peaceful, wrathful and dakini aspects of Padmasambhava and numerous other peaceful and wrathful yidams; in the Gelug tradition, Vajrabhairava and Guhyasamaja.

Generally speaking, completion of the Foundations enables us to practice all meditations involving the Developing and Fulfillment Stages.

Is it possible to reach full enlightenment simply by practicing these Four Foundations?

KALU RINPOCHE: Yes. In order to become a perfect Buddha, one must develop compassion. In this set of practices, compassion is developed by doing prostrations accompanied by engenderment of the enlightened attitude and the Four Immeasurables.

To become a perfect Buddha one must also understand emptiness. In each practice, the objects of meditation [i.e., the sources of refuge and so on] become inseparable from the meditator, and then the meditator lets his mind rest naturally. These are the profound means for realizing emptiness and Mahamudra.

The development of compassion and the realization of emptiness are the two requirements for achieving enlightenment. During the Four Foundation practices—particularly in Taking Refuge and Engendering the Enlightened Attitude and in the Guru-Yoga—these two are integrated.

NOTES

1. Kalu Rinpoche: November 4, 1974. Deshung Rinpoche: February 20, 1975. Chögyam Trungpa, Rinpoche: May 18, 1976.
2. Rinpoche was amused by my assumption that practice of the Four Foundations could be unsuccessful.

The Torch of Certainty

INVOCATION

To Marpa, Mila and Dagpo, three chiefs of the many siddhas,
To the glorious Kagyudpa, Dusum Khyenpa, who received their oral
  transmission,
To Vajradhara, holder of the Golden Rosary of Wish-Fulfilling Gems,
To the mighty Padma Nyinjay, I bow my head.[1]

Most excellent, perfect Buddha,
During rebirth, this lifetime and beyond,
Grant me, and each sentient being,
The blessing of realization of the true state of things.

1

The Four Ordinary Foundations

[In this opening chapter, four observations fundamental to the Buddhist view are presented. These are the "four thoughts which turn the mind to religion." We are urged to meditate on them—to think about what they mean and how they affect our lives. This contemplative practice is called the "Four Ordinary Foundations." It is presumed that once we have thoroughly internalized these thoughts, our interest will shift away from short-term worldly concerns and toward long-term religious ones, providing us with a basis for an ever-deepening involvement in religious practice. The four thoughts are:

1. "The Precious Human Birth," which instills an appreciation of the uniqueness and value of human existence. Human existence is unique because a human being's exceptional physical, verbal and mental endowment leaves him uniquely equipped to choose and follow a constructive course of action. Human birth is valuable because Buddhahood—supremely valuable, enlightened existence—may be more easily appreciated and realized by a human being than by any other.

These ideas are presented by first contrasting human capabilities with those of less fortunate beings ("the eight unfavorable states"), and our own ideal situation with that of others who are technically human but subject to certain dehumanizing circumstances ("the sixteen unfavorable conditions"). Then, the special boons ("the ten blessings") and responsibilities implicit in human existence are discussed.

2. "Impermanence" confronts us with the immanence of death and the utter groundlessness for our hopes that anything we now enjoy will outlast the moment. We are urged to use our fear of death as a motivation for religious practice. Religion is not presented as a foil for death but an antidote to the fearful experiences which usually precede, accompany and follow death.

3. "Action, Cause and Result." According to the Buddhist doctrine of karma, an "action" is anything one does, says or thinks. A "cause" is an emotion or intention which motivates an act. A "result" is an experience

arising from an act and its intention. Results are seldom experienced sooner
than the next lifetime and may be experienced much later.

Actions are considered cumulative, and each individual "carries" his
unique accumulation from life to life. This accumulation comprises the
inertia for cyclic existence, samsara. Samsara persists until we have experienced all the consequences of our acts and ceased to generate new ones.

Actions are grouped into two main classes, according to the nature of
their motivations and results. They are not seen as intrinsically good or
evil. "Samsaric" acts are those motivated by ignorance and the conflicting
emotions (*nyon-mongs-pa;* Skt. *klesha*) arising from ignorance. These result in rebirth. The particular type of rebirth we receive depends on whether
our acts have been largely "wholesome" or "unwholesome." "Ineffectual"
acts have negligible results. Acts may also be termed "meritorious" or "non-
meritorious," depending on whether they lead to a higher or lower samsaric
existence.

The other main class of actions, "actions which lead to liberation,"
consists of wholesome acts motivated by a desire for freedom from samsara.
Although happiness will result from all wholesome acts, samsaric happiness is not highly valued, as it is so fragile. Only liberation offers lasting
happiness.

Kongtrul's treatment of the doctrine of karma aims to convince us to
avoid unwholesome acts and cultivate wholesome ones. Although religious
practice will eventually destroy the emotional "roots" of samsaric action,
simple behavioral control is seen as a good beginning.

4. "The Shortcomings of Samsara" consolidates our growing conviction that liberation is the only worthwhile goal. Samsaric existence is sys-
tematically devalued. Every aspect is found to be replete with suffering and
devoid of lasting satisfaction. Even the human realm, previously extolled
as the most richly endowed, is shown to contain the greatest range of
suffering.]

PROLOGUE

Each of us has obtained a human body. Now we must learn the importance of "entering the Dharma's door" and turn our thoughts to the
Dharma.[2] For this to occur, we must have profound confidence based
on knowledge of the Precious Ones'[3] qualities. In addition to this confidence, we must be motivated by meditation on impermanence. If we do
not consider death and impermanence, our thoughts will not even begin
to turn to the Dharma. Relying also on a knowledge of the rarity [of

this human existence with its] opportunities and blessings, we begin
the basic practices, known as the Four Ordinary Foundations:

1. THE PRECIOUS HUMAN BIRTH

THE EIGHT UNFAVORABLE STATES OF EXISTENCE
IN WHICH INDIVIDUALS ARE DISADVANTAGED

First, meditate as follows: Consider the advantages of this rare human
existence with its eight opportunities and ten blessings, more precious
than a wish-fulfilling gem! Unlike ourselves, beings in the eight unfavorable states of existence are disadvantaged in the following ways:

1. Hell-beings suffer from heat and cold without the slightest
break.

2. Spirits are tormented by hunger and thirst.

3. Animals are stupid and confused, incapable of any understanding or knowledge.

4. Barbarians, born in those numerous borderlands untouched by
Dharma—which far outnumber Buddhist countries—cannot understand it.

5. Long-living gods of the Desire, Form, and Formless realms are
distracted by their love of worldly pleasures and samadhi, and have no
interest in the Dharma.[4]

6. Heretics and those who have a natural dislike for the Dharma
hold perverted views.

7. For those born in a dark age in which no Buddha comes and the
attributes of the Precious Ones are not renowned, the world is a desolate
place.

8. Mutes, said to be ignorant of the world of language, are dumb
and do not turn their thoughts to the Dharma.

None of these beings are fortunate enough to practice Dharma. All
of them are tormented by their past deeds. This is what it means to lack
leisure and opportunity.

You who have not been born into any of the eight unfavorable
states in which individuals[5] are disadvantaged, possess eight kinds of
opportunity. But though you have obtained a human body capable of
practicing Dharma, for your practice to be effective you must first be
free of the sixteen unfavorable conditions:

THE SIXTEEN UNFAVORABLE CONDITIONS

EIGHT UNFAVORABLE CONDITIONS BASED ON
PRESENT CIRCUMSTANCES

(1.) Because the five emotional poisons[6] are extremely potent, the individual is mentally disturbed, (2.) under the influence of corrupting companions, (3.) of false views and practice, or (4.) subject to extreme laziness. (5.) Due to previous bad deeds, a flood of obstacles now advances. (6.) The individual comes under others' control as a slave or servant, (7.) enters the Dharma out of non-religious concerns, such as fear of death or being without a regular source of food or clothing, or (8.) is insincerely involved in the Dharma for the sake of profit or renown.

EIGHT UNFAVORABLE CONDITIONS IN WHICH THE MIND
IS CUT OFF FROM THE DHARMA

(1.) The individual has great desire and attachment for his body, wealth, etc. (2.) Since his character is extremely coarse, all his acts are mean. (3.) No matter how much the teacher explains the miseries of the lower realms,[7] he is not frightened. (4.) No matter how much the teacher explains the great blessing of liberation, he has no faith in it. (5.) He naturally delights in unwholesome action. (6.) He is as much inclined to practice Dharma as a dog is to eat grass. (7.) He violates the "roots" of his Bodhisattva and other vows.[8] (8.) He breaks his sacred commitments[9] to his guru and religious companions.

Had you been subject to these sixteen unfavorable conditions, you would not have been influenced by the Dharma. Since that would have led you to act in a manner conducive to birth in the lower realms, rejoice in the fact that you are free of these unfavorable conditions, and learn to prevent their future occurrence.

THE TEN BLESSINGS OF THE PRECIOUS HUMAN BIRTH

THE FIVE PERSONAL BLESSINGS

(1.) You have obtained a human body, the reverse of the eight unfavorable states. (2.) You were born in a land to which, by virtue of the Dharma's words, Buddhism has spread. (3.) Since your eyes and

other sense organs are intact, you can understand whatever is taught.
(4.) Since you have "entered the door" of the Buddha Dharma and
have not become involved with heretics, your acts are not counterpro-
ductive. (5.) You have profound confidence in the Three Jewels.

THE FIVE BLESSINGS RECEIVED FROM OTHERS

(1.) Although the frequent periodic formation and dissolution of
the many realms of this universe makes it difficult for a Buddha to ever
appear, the Buddha Shakyamuni has come in our very age! (2.) Although Pratyekabuddhas[10] and others who did not preach the Dharma
have come, now this excellent one preaches the profound and extensive
holy Dharma. (3.) The Buddha's doctrine has not declined, but endures. (4.) It has many followers. (5.) Benevolent persons give food,
clothing and other necessities for maintaining conditions conducive to
religious practice, to those who, observing the vicissitudes of old age,
sickness and the like, are determined to leave samsara. Thus, those who
practice Dharma are not destitute.

WHY THE HUMAN BIRTH IS PRECIOUS

IT IS DIFFICULT TO OBTAIN

All sentient beings have a natural tendency to act harmfully;[11] few
act beneficially. Even among the few who do, the capacity for moral conduct required for acquisition of a human body is very rare. As a result,
beings of the three lower realms are as numerous as grains of soil in the
earth, while gods and human beings are exceedingly rare. Furthermore,
there are scarcely enough sentient beings with human bodies who live
by the Dharma to constitute a class of samsaric beings! It is impossible
to count all the insects living beneath a slab of rock. But it is possible
to count all the men living in an entire kingdom! So few human beings
practice Dharma; those who practice it correctly are as rare as daytime
stars.

IT IS EASILY LOST

This body is threatened by many potentially fatal circumstances
such as fire, flood, poison, weapons, malevolent planetary influences,
earthquakes, etc.—yet we never know when they will occur! Few con-

ditions favor its survival. Since the only difference between life and
death is the exhalation or inhalation of one rasping breath, this body is
more easily destroyed than a bubble.

A precious human body like this one will never be found again.
Do not let it go to waste! If you had an animal's body, the means to
achieve enlightenment would be beyond your reach. Although you would
not know how to recite one "Mani,"[12] you would have the power to do
the kind of deeds which lead to rebirth in the lower realms.

IT HAS A GREAT OBJECTIVE

Thanks to this human body, we have the ability to achieve complete
Buddhahood: this is its great objective. Up to now, we have not valued
it very highly, but spent it in vain. Worldly men, concerned with their
well-being, can deal with hardships they encounter in business, etc. But
when *we* encounter hardships in our struggle for life's ultimate goal—
liberation—we are completely lacking in energy. We are degenerate,
dissipated, and beguiled by Mara.[13] From this day on, meditate repeatedly
on the thought, "I must exert myself exclusively in the practice of religion! I must accomplish life's objective!"

Generally speaking, one who is inclined to do particular types of
deeds is called a "karma-carrier." A "karma-carrier" who practiced
Dharma in his previous life is now inclined to place his confidence in
the Dharma and the guru. This is a sign of the reawakening of his [past]
"white" deeds. But one who acts harmfully in this life will, at rebirth,
be "carried" to the lower realms, not to a human body.

From the *Kshitigarbha sutra*:[14]

There are ten kinds of samsaric beings for whom true human birth is
difficult to obtain. Who are they? They are: (1.) those who have not culti-
vated the sources of wholesome action;[15] (2.) who have not accumulated
a quantity of merit; (3.) who follow the ways of corrupting companions;
(4.) for whom conflicting emotions persist; (5.) who do not fear suffering
in future lives; (6.) who are very disturbed by conflicting emotions; (7.)
who are lazy and careless about Dharma practice; (8.) who embrace
Buddha's teachings but do not follow them; (9.) who adhere to perverted
views, or (10.) who thoroughly believe in them.

Beware of these! To say, "Since I understand the great importance
of this human body, I am great! I am learned! I am nobly born! I am
good!," constitutes contempt for others. Take notice and stop! Since all

living beings possess the Buddha-potential,[16] it is wrong to despise even a mere insect.

It is said that when the tendency to condemn others has fully matured, in this life you will lose what you cherish. In the next, you will either be born among the spirits or as an enslaved human being. Since ordinary beings [like ourselves] lack the supersensible cognitions[17] [of spiritually advanced beings], we do not know who may be an Arhat and who a Bodhisattva, how such beings may be teaching Dharma, or what special methods they may be using to help sentient beings.

Being ignorant yourself, do not judge others! Since it is said that one who despises a Bodhisattva will suffer the agonies of hell for many kalpas, do not discount the seriousness of even one unpleasant joke at another's expense.

The type of person whose faith vacillates, whose insight is limited, who is easily led astray by companions and is frightened by profound teachings will develop gradually, trained in a gradual path closely guided by a guru of skillful methods. Before he may be instructed in "seeing" and "meditating"[18] he must amass and integrate the Two Accumulations.[19]

But the type of person capable of instantaneous illumination—whose insight is expansive, whose compassion is great, who is filled with unbending faith and devotion, who lacks desire and attachment, who thinks only of the Dharma and especially delights in profound doctrine—such a person merely requires a teaching which immediately points out the ultimate nature of reality, and dispenses with the visualizations and other practices employed by the "path of means."[20] So it has been said!

2.   IMPERMANENCE

According to the Kadampa school, these are the five basic thoughts comprising meditation on impermanence:

1.   "THINK THAT NOTHING LASTS."

First, the external world is produced, then it persists. Finally, destroyed by fire and flood, nothing remains of it, not even specks of dust!

Last year, this year, yesterday, today, even months and years, are quickly used up.

All living beings, the contents of the world, are impermanent. First you were an infant; later a child; then a youth; now an old man. Each day, each month quickly brings us closer and closer to death. Meditate on all this, and think, "What should I do?"

2. "THINK THAT MANY OTHER PEOPLE HAVE DIED."

Remember that although there are those living who are older, younger or the same age as yourself, there are many more who are dead. This one died; that one, too, turned to dust. First they grew old, then they died! The two always seem to go together. Often, happy, joyful people die so suddenly that they have no time to think or reminisce.

Sometimes, even without dying, prominent men fall; the lowly become prominent. A beggar becomes rich; a rich man becomes a beggar, and so on.

Since absolutely nothing in your daily experience transcends impermanence, at some time it is bound to affect you also. So right now, while there is still time, think, "I really must practice Dharma strenuously!"

3. "THINK REPEATEDLY OF THE MANY CIRCUMSTANCES WHICH MIGHT CAUSE DEATH."

Since there are a great many circumstances which might cause death—such as avalanches, falling objects, thunder or lightning, strokes, internal ailments, and the like—we do not know how or when we will die. But as long as we have accumulated karma, death is inevitable. Even our food, clothing, friends, attendants and servants may become the cause of our own death. We never know!

Since you do not know when you will die, now earnestly meditate on the thought, "What will happen to me?"

The *Bodhisattva-pitaka*[21] lists the nine causes of sudden death:

1. eating unwholesome food
2. eating when you are full
3. eating before digesting the previous meal
4. not eliminating at the right time
5. while ill, neither heeding the nurse nor taking his prescriptions
6. being possessed by a fierce disease-demon
7. taking an emetic and vomiting
8. impulsively engaging in violence
9. indulging in sex without restraint.

Beware of these!

4. "MEDITATE ON WHAT WILL HAPPEN
AT THE HOUR OF DEATH."

The coming of death is never desired, but always unwanted and unin-
vited. An individual who has done harm is terrified. In his dying hours,
he experiences incredibly intense pain and the shuddering sensation of
life being cut off. He sees apparitions everywhere. He cannot control
his body or mind, so whatever comes to mind becomes immeasurable.
Because the state of mind at death is very potent, even one careless unwholesome thought will assure his rebirth in the lower realms. Since
[your own rebirth] depends on your present behavior, from now on, get
into the habit of practicing Dharma!

Since you cannot reverse a used-up lifetime, even with a Buddha's
help—to say nothing of the impotence of methods like divination, exorcism,[22] medical treatment, scripture-reading, or offering of food or
money—there is simply no way to escape death. So instead of grieving
later, set to work now!

5. "THINK ABOUT WHAT HAPPENS AFTER DEATH."

Think: From the moment of death, even a world-ruler[23] lacks the power
to take along one mouthful of food, one article of his clothing, one penny
of his money. He cannot even take his most lowly servant.

After your corpse has been wrapped in a shroud and bound with
rope, everyone will turn away from it in disgust. A few days later, not
even "the remains" will be left.[24]

Lacking mental control, like a wind-blown feather you travel the
treacherous path of the terrifying bardo.[25] You wander aimlessly in an
unfamiliar world, followed by your "black" and "white" deeds.

There is simply no way to undo the harm you have done, but the
holy Dharma and wholesome action will help you. Now, meditate, "If
I do not practice strenuously at this time, after death [it will be too late]
for anyone to grant me an extension!"

In brief, there is nothing for you to do but practice Dharma from
now on. You cannot simply "let it be!" You must make it part of your
very existence. You must meditate on making it part of your existence.
Once you have achieved stability, you must become the type of person
who will be happy at death, and whom others will venerate, saying, "He
was a true religious man!"

Everywhere, people are crying, "A man has died! Oh no! Oh, guru,

help him!" but you never think that death will stealthily and quickly
overtake you, too! You know that you will die some day, but you imagine
that it will not happen for a long time.

Intellectually you know that death may come at any time, but you
are not really convinced of this. When things go wrong, you are distracted by samsara's appearances[26] and act contrary to the Dharma. Since
such behavior cannot do you any good, you have already wasted the
greater part of this lifetime!

Think: "Right now, since death is at my door, I must forget about
things like food, money, clothing and fame. There is no time to spare!"
and fit yourself, body, speech and mind into the path of the Dharma.

When you consider those who simply take it easy, who lack mental
discipline and do not take seriously the immanence of death, you should
think—"What can they be thinking? Oh, no! They are not afraid of
death!"—but keep your own mind focused on it.

3.   ACTION, CAUSE AND RESULT

Since the doctrine of "action, cause and result" contains the fundamental message of the limitless collection of Buddha's teachings, it is
exceedingly profound and extensive. Only a person who has reached
the "one-valueness"[27] realization will have cleared up his doubts about
"action, cause and result." Ordinary people will not really understand
it. But generally, this sums it all up: A wholesome cause yields a pleasant
result; an unwholesome cause yields an unpleasant result.

First we will discuss the causes and results of samsara, then the
causes and results of liberation.

ACTION WHICH LEADS TO SAMSARA

The accumulation of bad deeds is the root of suffering in samsara. Conflicting emotions are to blame for bad deeds. Ignorance which holds the
self dear is to blame for conflicting emotions. Mental darkness is the
root of ignorance and of all conflicting emotions. Because of mental
darkness, we do not know where samsara comes from, what its nature
is, what types of actions, causes and results are helpful, what types are
harmful, and so on: We are in the dark! For example, if the teacher
explains [the nature of reality], after listening and thinking about what
he said, we may reach a conceptual understanding. But just like day-
dreaming of a land we have never visited, when we apply conceptual

designations to [ultimate reality] which is not a "thing,"[28] we are simply playing with concepts.

By this same process, we apply the designation "self" to that which is not [a solid, separate self], and then cling to that "self." Based on this, doubt about ultimate reality[29] and many other perverted attitudes arise. Then, attachment to anything which supports the "self," such as the body, wealth, etc., and consequently pride, jealousy and greed spring up. Aversion to what is "other," and consequently, burning anger, malice and the like erupt.

If you are free of [mental darkness, attachment and aversion,] the three emotional poisons, your acts will not accumulate. Since results do not come about without actions, you must do what you can to dig up these three roots of wandering in samsara.

To summarize the topic of "action which leads to samsara": Non-meritorious action, grouped into "ten unwholesome acts," leads to rebirth in the lower realms. Meritorious action, including generosity and so on, if it is not motivated by the desire to achieve nirvana, leads to rebirth in the higher realms as a god or human being. Imperturbable action,[30] such as samadhi which involves clinging, leads to rebirth [as a god] in the Form or Formless realm.

In brief, until our propensities for conceptualization have been exhausted, this continuous pattern of karmic accumulation will not be disturbed, and the illusion which is samsara will be perpetuated. A stupid person who, since his meditation is blank, says, "Ah! I have understood [the ultimate nature of mind]. I don't have to worry about my acts and their consequences," is a great thief of the doctrine.[31]

UNWHOLESOME ACTION

These are the ten unwholesome acts:

1. Do not consciously take the life of any living being, even an ant, for when it comes to life there is no "big" or "small."[32]

2. Do not secretly take another's property when it hasn't been offered to you.

3. Do not indulge in sexual intercourse with an inappropriate partner: one who has taken vows or is married to someone else; at an inappropriate time: when your wife is pregnant; in an inappropriate place: near a guru, shrine-room or stupa; or in an inappropriate manner: orally or anally. These are the four unchaste acts. All of the above constitute the three unwholesome physical acts.

4. Do not consciously lie: that is, say what is untrue.

5. Do not slander: that is, say things which will promote discord.

6. Do not speak ill of others: that is, call a man a thief or half-wit, or hurt his feelings by cruelly exposing his faults.

7. Do not engage in idle chatter about military or business matters, about women, or engage in frivolous songs, dances, jokes, etc. These are the four unwholesome verbal acts.

8. Do not covet someone else's money, wife, reputation, etc., thinking, "Oh, if only *I* had that!"

9. Do not resent others: that is, be displeased by their happiness or good fortune.

10. Do not hold perverted views: that is, doubt the existence of past or future lives; of action, cause and result; or of the special qualities of the Precious Ones. These are the three unwholesome mental acts.

To sum up, when each of these ten unwholesome acts has fully matured, you will be reborn in the lower realms. Even if you are reborn in the human realm, since you have taken life, your life will be cut short. Since you have stolen, you will be poor. Since all these acts lead to many sorrows, simply avoid them! Dissuade others from committing them. Regret those which have been committed.

WHOLESOME ACTION

This is the opposite of unwholesome action.

1. Instead of killing, save lives.

2. Instead of stealing, distribute your own food and money.

3. Preserve moral conduct whether anyone is watching or not.

4. Speak truthfully.

5. Patch up quarrels caused by slander.

6. Use gentle words.

[7. Discuss worthwhile topics].

8. Rejoice in the good fortune of others.

9. Think only of their benefit.

10. When you hear the views of another sect, do not denounce them but simply maintain your faith in the Buddha's words.

These are the ten wholesome acts. Do your best to carry them out. Bid others to do the same. Rejoice at those which have already been done. As a result, you will live long in the higher realms, possessing many comforts such as great wealth.

NEITHER WHOLESOME NOR UNWHOLESOME ACTION

You might "kill time" walking, moving, sleeping or sitting: ineffectual acts which are neither wholesome nor harmful, and which mature into neither good nor bad experiences. But since such actions simply waste this human life, instead of throwing your ability away in idle amusements, make a conscious effort to devote your time exclusively to wholesome action. Avoid carelessly committing even minor harmful acts, recalling that "Even a small amount of poison may be fatal." Do not underestimate the power of even a minor wholesome act, recalling that "Enough grains of barley will eventually fill the bag."

THE EIGHT HEAVENLY QUALITIES

You should develop a character endowed with the renowned "eight heavenly qualities," the basis for the accumulation of a great deal of merit in future lives. This includes: (1.) Long life, since you have stopped harming others; (2.) a pleasing form, since you have offered lamps, clothing and so on; (3.) a noble birth, since you have humbly paid homage to the guru and religious companions; (4.) the power of wealth, since you have given poor learned men, the sick and the needy all they wanted; (5.) authoritative speech, since you have only spoken constructively; (6.) great power and influence, since you have made fine offerings and prayers to the Precious Ones and your parents; (7.) a male body, since you have befriended men and saved animals from castration, and (8.) all types of strength in abundance, since you have helpfully befriended others without hoping to fulfill religious obligations. Cultivate [behavior which] will give you these qualities.

Once you lack all desire for samsara, you must learn to abandon its cause: unwholesome action. And whether anyone is watching or not, do not cheat in the performance of these and other wholesome meritorious acts or in the preservation of vows, sacred commitments and other wholesome acts which lead to liberation.

ACTION WHICH LEADS TO LIBERATION

To achieve liberation, you must first be one who adheres unfailingly to moral conduct because he is absolutely determined to leave samsara. Consequently, you will achieve the samadhi in which the attention remains one-pointed. As a result, through insight which realizes "non-self," you will know the general and specific characteristics of impermanence, suffering, emptiness etc. Your previously accumulated deeds, which now obstruct [spiritual progress], will be removed. They will not recur. When your suffering is finally exhausted, you will rest in the realization beyond extremes which is called "liberation." Achieving "liberation" or "nirvana" does not entail going to another place or becoming someone else.

SUMMARY

In brief: The result of wholesome action is happiness; the result of unwholesome action is suffering, and nothing else. These results are not interchangeable: when you plant buckwheat, you get buckwheat; when you plant barley, you get barley.

ACTIONS AND INTENTIONS

Killing a living being as an offering to the Precious Ones, or beating and insulting someone "for his own good" are examples of acts "white" in intention but "black" in application. Building a temple out of desire for fame, or getting an education out of an urge to compete, are examples of acts "black" in intention but "white" in application. Along with pretending to be a monk out of fear of embarrassment—all these are said to be unwholesome acts which must be rejected as if they were poison. This being so, what must we say about acts which are absolutely unwholesome?? Be content with wholesome acts; confess[33] harmful acts, etc. If you do not destroy them with these antidotes, the deeds you have done will mature only for yourself, and no one else. They cannot possibly be lost or used up, even after many kalpas. Furthermore, actions always increase, even those arising from the slightest motivation. You might kill out of fierce anger or save a doomed man out of pure benevolence. Major acts increase without measure. Even the most weakly motivated wholesome or harmful word or deed increases a hundred or a thousandfold. If you yourself have not acted or had intentions, it is impossible for someone else's acts to affect you. Thus, if you can live by the doctrine of "cause and result" which was expounded by the Buddha himself, it will be absolutely impossible for you to be thrown into the lower realms, however bad others may be.

Examine every one of your own faults, but no one else's. See others as pure. Since this is the root of the entire doctrine of "action and re-sult," it was highly prized by the great Kagyudpas.[34]

4. THE SHORTCOMINGS OF SAMSARA

HELL-BEINGS

THE EIGHT HOT HELLS

For those born in the eight hot hells, all the mountains and valleys are blazing red-hot iron. The rivers and lakes are molten copper and bronze. The trees send a rain of swords and other sharp weapons. The inhabitants enjoy not a moment's rest, but are incessantly slaughtered by wild beasts and horrible demons.

Life in the Avici hell is the most intensely painful of all. Even the Bhagavan[35] cannot bear to speak of its miseries. For it is said, when he does, the merciful Bodhisattvas vomit blood and come dangerously close to death.

THE EIGHT COLD HELLS

For those born in the cold hells, all the mountains and valleys are snow and ice. Due to the bitterly cold wind and storms, their bodies are covered with tiny cracks. Even before their billion-year life is over, they die again and again only to be instantly reborn and undergo the same suffering once more.

MISCELLANEOUS HELLS

The miseries experienced by those in the "occasional" and "neigh-boring" hells are as bad as the rest.

SPIRITS

The spirits cannot find any food or drink. Increasingly tormented by hunger and thirst but finding only mucus and feces, they are wearied by their hopeless search. Naked, they burn in summer and freeze in winter. When it rains, live coals fall and burn them. They see water as pus. Flames shoot from their dislocated joints. They continually fight and beat each other, each one thinking the other his enemy. They may live for fifteen-thousand human years.

ANIMALS

Animals in the sea are as crowded as grains of malting barley. They survive by eating each other. Constantly tormented by fear, they wander about, carried by waves.

Even animals who live in more spacious mountain habitats are un-happy, always fearing some enemy's approach. They kill each other.

Even the domesticated ones are hitched to ploughs or killed for meat and hides. They are stupid. In addition to the misery of stupidity, they suffer as much from heat and cold as do the hell-beings and spirits.

GODS

The gods of the Desire realm are distracted by the pleasant lives they lead and do not think about the Dharma. Seven god-days before their lives are over, they perceive five different death-omens.[36] They see their future birthplaces in the hells and elsewhere and experience the misery of their own downfall, like fish writhing on hot sand.

When they have exhausted their store of good deeds, even the gods of the four dhyanas[37] and the Formless realm experience a weakening of samadhi and gradually fall.

ASURAS

Since asuras are naturally envious of the splendor of the gods, they do nothing but fight with them. Their accumulated merit is weak, and they dislike the Dharma. They are defeated in battle and suffer intense pain when slaughtered.

HUMANS

The misery of birth in this human realm resembles that of a little bird carried off by a hawk. The misery of aging is like that of a mother camel losing her calf. The misery of illness is like that of a guilty man going to prison. The misery of death is like that of a man pursued by an execu-tioner. Each of these includes five kinds of misery.

THE FIVE MISERIES OF BIRTH

Due to the violent pain which accompanies it, (1.) birth entails the misery of being born. Because anyone who is born has "sown the seeds" of conflicting emotions, (2.) birth may entail the misery of receiving a low status. Because old age, sickness and death come after it, (3.) birth is the ground for suffering. Because the conflicting emotions gradually expand and we accumulate actions, (4.) birth is the ground for the conflicting emotions. Because of momentariness and impermanence, (5.) birth implies the misery of being powerless in the face of destruction.

THE FIVE MISERIES OF AGING

The miseries of aging include: (1.) fading of the complexion, (2.) deterioration of the form, (3.) dissipation of energy, (4.) impairment of the senses and (5.) decline of wealth.

THE FIVE MISERIES OF ILLNESS

The miseries of illness include: (1.) the increase of frustration and anxiety, (2.) the body's natural changes, (3.) the inability to enjoy pleasant things, (4.) the need to rely on what is unpleasant and (5.) the approaching separation from life.

THE FIVE MISERIES OF DEATH

The miseries of death include: (1.) separation from wealth, (2.) from influence, (3.) from attendants and friends, (4.) and even from your own body, and (5.) violent anguish.

THE MISERY OF NOT FINDING WHAT YOU SEEK

Although you strive so hard for it that you lose all regard for the injury, suffering or malicious talk you inflict on others, you do not obtain the food, money or fame you desire. This is the misery of not finding what you seek.

THE MISERY OF NOT RETAINING WHAT YOU HAVE

Dreading the approach of an enemy, thief or a violent robber; being left with only the stars for a hat and the frost for boots; being exhausted from too much work; worrying about your ability to protect [your dependents]; and worrying that your enemies will not [be punished]: this is the misery of not retaining what you have.

THE MISERY OF SEPARATION FROM WHAT IS DEAR

Loss of essential persons such as parents, siblings, servants, students and so on; decline of wealth and power; loss of a large sum of money; anxiety about slander you have incurred through bad deeds or another's jealousy: this is the misery of separation from what is dear.

THE MISERY OF ENCOUNTERING THE UNDESIRABLE

Encountering illness, dangerous enemies, the arm of the law, a murderer, a bad reputation, evil rumors; incurring punishment in return for help; having lazy servants, and so on: this is the misery of encountering the undesirable.

The above eight categories of misery pertain chiefly to human beings.

THREE TYPES OF MISERY COMMON TO ALL SAMSARIC BEINGS[38]

THE MISERY OF MISERY ITSELF

In brief, the miseries experienced by beings in the lower realms and the pain of disease, malicious gossip etc., experienced by gods and men constitute the misery of misery itself.

THE MISERY OF CHANGE

When you lead a wealthy, peaceful existence, life seems very pleasant. But soon, because of impermanence, the misery of change arrives.

THE MISERY OF ALL CONDITIONED EXISTENCE

The two kinds of misery mentioned above are grounded in the fact that five skandhas[39] have come together. This is the misery latent in all conditioned existence.

Finding their foothold in the five skandhas, the many kinds of misery of the three realms arise. Thus, no matter how high or low your state of birth, you cannot avoid samsara's very nature: the three types of misery! Even if your life seems happy and you possess a [healthy] body, a house, money, friends and servants—these are merely misery in disguise. They are like food offered to a nauseated man or a hangman's feast for a condemned prisoner.

Turn your back on longing! Root out attachment! Destroy desire [for conditioned existence] from its foundation! Reflect on the great blessing of liberation! This is the opposite of thinking about samsara's shortcomings. Then, energetically apply the methods for achieving enlightenment [which are presented below].

CONCLUSION

Generally speaking, the Four Ordinary Foundations are found in all instructions in the graded path to enlightenment. Our version is based on Atisha's system, known as "the graded path for the three types of religious aspirants." This was elaborated by Nyam-me Dagpo, who merged the two streams of the Kadampa and Mahamudra systems.

If you do not apply these four with some fortitude, instead of bolstering the meditative practices [which follow], you will only strengthen the "eight worldly dharmas."[40]

The root of the entire Dharma is mental rejection of the concerns of this life. But all your religious practice up to now has not destroyed your attachment for this life. Your mind has not turned away from desire. You have not given up longing for relatives, friends, attendants and servants. You have not even slightly curtailed your desire for food, clothing and conversation. You have missed the whole point of applying wholesome action; the stream of your existence is on the wrong course! You do not consider the extent to which your practice has weakened the conflicting emotions, but only the number of months and years you have been working at it. You examine others' faults but not your own. You are proud of every good quality you possess. Your thoughts are lost in trivialities such as your reputation and amusements. You indulge in meaningless chatter. You imagine that you have integrated religious and worldly achievements when in fact not even one of these goals has been met. You have failed from the start to think about impermanence and so are in the clutches of your own brutish mentality.

The Excellent One of Drikhung has said: "The [Four Ordinary] Foundations are more profound than the actual practice [of Mahamudra].[41] It follows that it is better to instill these Four Foundations in the stream of your existence, even to a limited extent, than to practice all the recitations and meditations of the four tantras in current use.

An individual who practices Dharma in a half-hearted manner is cheating both himself and others and wasting his human life.

In short, if you lack the determination to leave samsara, all the meditation [you may practice in your mountain retreat] will accumulate nothing but a pile of feces on the mountainside! So, consider the miseries of samsara and the uncertainty of the time of death. Then, no matter how varied your concerns, narrow them down!

They say that the faith of a person who has begun to travel the religious path will diminish if Mara has thrown obstacles in his way. Examination of the guru's or spiritual friend's[42] faults is a sign of Mara's embrace. Such a person notices serious faults in most people who practice Dharma, associates with ordinary people,[43] is unconcerned with strenuous application of the teachings, is satisfied with worldly pleasures and lacks devotion and reverence for the Precious Ones. Such a person should think about the positive qualities of the guru and the Precious Ones and learn to see those who practice Dharma as pure. Seeing bad qualities in others indicates that your own acts have been impure. It is just like seeing your own dirty face in a mirror.

Do not associate with ordinary people or listen to their talk! Remember the shortcomings of worldly pleasures! Generally speaking, if you have no faith you will not develop "white" qualities. Hence, faith must precede all religious practice. Although there are many kinds of faith, deep confidence and sincere respect for the Precious Ones are included in all of them.

Experiencing the vicissitudes of life and death, illness, demons, and accidents; and listening to the spiritual biographies of the great ones and stories of the Buddha's previous lives will promote the development of faith. Engender faith by reviewing them in your thoughts daily.

Some people seem to have great faith while in the presence of their guru, but lose it when separated from him. Sometimes they have faith; later it is gone. When they receive desired teachings or gifts, or are tormented by disease-demons or other misfortunes, they have great faith. Afterwards, they have none. They have no heartfelt confidence in one particular root-guru or one profound teaching but often discard one in favor of another.

Reject such practices. Learn to develop unwavering faith. Stop looking to external things. Internalize [the foregoing teachings]. Then when some religious qualities arise in the stream of your existence, you will truly comprehend these instructions. You will be absolutely certain about the Dharma. If you then consider your guru's kindness, you will experience spontaneous devotion and reverence for him. As a result, all the positive qualities associated with the religious path will spontaneously arise without any effort on your part.

NOTES

1. Marpa (1012-97), his disciple Milarepa (1040-1123) and his disciple Dagpo or Gampopa (1079-1153) were important figures in early Buddhist Tibet. Upon their work, Dusum Khyenpa (1110-93) founded the Karma Kagyud sect. He is recognized as its first Karmapa, or head.

The "Golden Rosary of Wish-Fulfilling Gems" is the Mahamudra lineage whose source is the Buddha Vajradhara (Dorje Chang), the Karma Kagyudpa's symbol of supreme enlightenment.

Situ Padma Nyinjay (1774-1853) was Kongtrul's root-guru or chief spiritual teacher.

2. I.e., Buddhist doctrine.

3. The Three Jewels: Buddha, Dharma and Sangha. See chapter 2.

4. Gods of the Desire realm are attached to worldly pleasures. Gods of the other two realms cling to the subtler delights of samadhi (meditation). See *Kosa,* chap. 3, pp. 6–7, 172–73; chap. 8, 127–218.

5. *rang-rgyud*: "stream of being." Buddhism does not regard the individual as a permanent, unitary 'self' (Sanskrit: *atman*) encased in a mortal body, but as a constantly changing "stream" of psycho-physical events.

6. Pride, desire-attachment, aversion, jealousy, and confusion or bewilderment.

7. The realms of hell-beings, spirits and animals.

8. All vows (*sdom-pa*) include an essential clause or "root." Violating this breaks the vow.

9. *dam-tshig.* All sacred oaths and promises, called "vows" in the Mahayana, are called "sacred commitments" or "sacred bonds" in the Vajrayana. These include: 1. the bond or special relationship to the guru which is formed when instruction or empowerment is received from him; 2. the bond formed between an aspirant and any yidam (see chap. 2, n. 10) upon the former's receipt of empowerment. Thereafter, that yidam and his meditations will be the major focus of the aspirant's practice.

10. A Pratyekabuddha is one who meditates to achieve enlightenment for himself alone. In the Mahayana, he is considered inferior to a Bodisattva, who works to help all beings reach Buddhahood.

11. This tendency is based upon ignorance (*ma-rig-pa;* Skt. *avidya*),

the fundamental, defining condition of sentient beings. Ignorance gives rise to the three types of emotionality (*nyon-mongs-pa;* Skt. *klesha*): attachment, aversion and bewilderment, which inspire harmful acts.

    12. I.e., the mantra, "Oṁ Mani Padme Hūṁ."

    13. Mara: 1. personification of factors which hinder or obstruct religious practice; 2. a demon who endangers faith (Lama); 3. the four Maras, described by H. V. Guenther as, "... certain limiting factors which ... have a deadening influence on life." *Jewel Ornament,* pp. 199–200.

    For a fine study on Mara, see T. O. Ling, *Buddhism and the Mythology of Evil.* London: Allen and Unwin, 1962.

    14. *'Phags-pa sa'i snying-po'i mtshan brgya-rtsa-brgyad gzung-shags dang bcas-pa. bKa'-'gyur,* P. 327, 506. A devotional work.

    15. Non-attachment, non-aversion and mental clarity.

    16. See D. S. Ruegg, *Théorie du tathagatagarbha et du gotra.* Paris: Ecole Francaise D'Extrême-Orient, 1969.

    17. *mngon-shes;* Skt. *abhijna.*

        There are six supersensible cognitions and faculties: ... miraculous powers (such as multiplying oneself, walking through walls and so on); hearing human and divine voices far and near; knowing others' thoughts; recollection of former lives; the vision of beings passing away and then reincarnating; and the awareness that all disturbing elements have lost their power of keeping us on low planes.

    H. V. Guenther, *Jewel Ornament,* p. 52.

    18. "Seeing" (*lta;* Skt. *darshana*): perception of the nature of things. "Meditating" (*sgom;* Skt. *bhavana*): attentive concentration to that which has been perceived. See *Jewel Ornament,* p. 84.

    19. 1. Accumulation of Merit (*bsod-nams-kyi tshogs*); 2. Accumulation of Awareness (*ye-shes-kyi tshogs*). "Merit" refers to meritorious action. "Awareness" is transcending awareness: seeing things as they are. This twofold accumulation is a prerequisite to higher meditative practice. See chapter 4.

    20. *thabs-lam;* Skt. *upaya-marga:* the usual approach to enlightenment, a gradual path employing visualizations, prayers and mantras, and so on. (Lama)

    21. *Byang-chub sems-dpa'i sde-snod.* Early Mahayana sutra containing the doctrine of the Six Perfections. Part of the Ratnakuta group, *bKa'.,* P. 760 (12).

    22. Divination (*mo*) and exorcism (*gto*) were standard Tibetan medical practices. First the demon causing the illness would be identified by divination, then it would be exorcised. (LPL)

    23. *'khor-los sgyur-pa'i rgyal-po;* Skt. *cakravartin.* See chapter 4, n. 19.

    24. This is because the corpse has been left for the vultures, a common practice in the mountainous regions of Tibet. (LPL)

    25. The bardo is the state experienced between death and entry into a womb, during which time the ordinary person acts in ways which reflect his past deeds and is unable to exercise free will. This drivenness and helplessness is symbolized by the feather (the individual) tossed about by the wind

(of karma). An individual who is prepared for these experiences is not help-less and may attain enlightenment directly from the bardo instead of being conceived anew. See Francesca Fremantle and Chögyam Trungpa's transla-tion, *The Tibetan Book of the Dead.* Berkeley: Shambhala, 1975.

26. *'jig-rten-gyi snang-ba*: the distorted ways things ordinarily appear to us, due to our ignorance and emotionality. Especially heightened in times of stress. (Lama)

27. *ro-gcig*: third of the four stages in Mahamudra realization. Ac-cording to H. V. Guenther:

> One-valueness is the experience of everything that appears as nothing, though not in the sense that appearance is mere illusion and that . . . there is no need for serious action. On the contrary, one-valueness is the spontaneous interest in the several situations of life which man encounters. This interest has been purified of all vested interests through the preceding phases of the concentrative process, and hence is more suited for beneficial activity. However . . . this stage is not the final realization. *Naropa*, p. 195.

28. Ultimate reality is not a "thing" which can be understood through concepts. It is empty (*stong-pa;* Skt. *shunya*), or open.

29. Doubt about ultimate reality, i.e., about the ultimate nature of reality, leads ordinary people to look upon the various loosely-connected, ever-changing factors of their existence as if these comprised a solid, unitary, permanent "self" or ego. This misapprehension promotes emotionality, which leads to unwholesome acts in support of that nonexistent "self."

30. *mi-gyo-pa'i las;* Skt. *aninjya-karma*. See *Kosa*, chap. 3, p. 84; chap. 4, p. 106.

31. One who mistakes the mental blankness of fruitless meditation for realization of emptiness or openness, the ultimate nature of mind (*sems-gyi gnas-lugs*: ultimate nature of reality in the mentalistic terminology of the Kagyudpas), distorts or "steals" the spirit of the doctrine. (Lama)

32. Refers especially to animals. It is more serious to kill a human be-ing than an animal. (Lama)

33. For Confession (*shags*), see chapter 2, n. 47, and chapter 3, pp. 84–85.

34. Eminent Kagyudpa gurus of the past.

35. Lit.: "Conquerer", i.e., the Buddha.

36. ". . . his dress becomes soiled; his garlands of flowers fade; per-spiration breaks forth from his arm-pits; an evil smell rises from his body and he is dissatisfied with his seat." H. V. Guenther, *Jewel Ornament*, p. 68.

37. I.e., the Form realm.

38. The first is painful experience itself; the second is anxiety based on the transitoriness of pleasant experience; the third is the misery "latent" in samsaric life, since all beings therein will eventually experience all the types of misery explained in this section.

39. Five skandhas (lit., "aggregates"): the five psycho-physical con-stituents of an individual life or, more generally, five factors present in any moment of relational existence. These include internal as well as external

factors, i.e., 1. form and color, 2. feeling, 3. sensation-ideation, 4. motivation and 5. consciousness. See H. V. Guenther's *Jewel Ornament*, p. 199, and Chögyam Trungpa's *Myth of Freedom*. Berkeley: Shambhala, 1976, pp. 20–23.

40. *chos-brgyad*: the concerns of a worldly person: 1. profit, 2. loss, 3. fame, 4. notoriety, 5. slander, 6. praise, 7. happiness, 8. misery.

41. For the beginner, these Foundations are far more accessible and therefore more potent than the advanced Mahamudra meditations. Therefore, they are essential prerequisites for Mahamudra practice. (Lama)

42. I.e., religious teacher or advisor.

43. I.e., non-religious people.

2 FIRST OF THE FOUR
SPECIAL FOUNDATIONS

Taking Refuge and Engendering
the Enlightened Attitude

[After internalizing the "four thoughts which turn the mind to religion," the aspirant takes refuge and engenders the enlightened attitude, the two rituals dealt with in this chapter. The heart of the first ritual is the refuge vow recited in the visualized presence of the six sources of refuge, i.e., Buddhist doctrine and the five types of enlightened beings. In making this commitment to strive toward Buddhahood and become like these enlightened beings, the aspirant becomes a Buddhist and gains their protection from the vicissitudes of samsara.

In this tradition, a further ritual, Engendering the Enlightened Attitude, always accompanies Taking Refuge. The core of this ritual is the Bodhisattva vow in which the individual resolves to devote himself fully to the liberation of all beings. In making this resolution, he becomes a Bodhisattva: a socially-oriented Buddha-to-be.

The actual practice of Taking Refuge and Engendering the Enlightened Attitude involves the following steps:

1. Sitting cross-legged before an icon of the sources of refuge, visualizing them arranged in the refuge tree and chanting a liturgical description of this scene, while imagining that all beings are doing the same.

2. Reciting the refuge vow and performing full prostrations, each a total of 111,111 times.

3. Reciting the Bodhisattva vow and related prayers.

4. Dissolving the visualization and letting the mind rest.

5. Dedicating merit.]

TAKING REFUGE

VISUALIZATION

After you have practiced the Four Ordinary Foundations, begin the first

of the Four Special Foundations, "Taking Refuge." Build up the following visualization [as you recite the liturgy].[1]

On a wide spacious plain in a pure land is the Nananemtegnapar
forest. In the middle of a rich, green, flowering meadow is a lake whose
water has eight fine attributes. The lake is inhabited by heavenly birds
whose songs are most pleasing to the ear. In the midst of this lake stands
a wish-fulfilling tree laden with leaves, flowers and fruit of precious gems.
Its single-rooted trunk divides into five branches like a parasol, one point-
ing in each of the four directions and one at the center, [pointing
straight up].[2]

GURUS

Resting on the central branch at the point at which all the branches
converge is a jewelled throne upheld by eight lions. The throne is covered with heavenly silks on which rest a thousand-petal lotus and, above
it, a full moon [lying flat]. [On top of this] sits your root-guru in the
form of Vajradhara (Dorje Chang), his body blue as the autumn sky.
Vajradhara has one face and two hands crossed at his breast; the right
hand holds a golden vajra and the left a silver bell.[3] His gaze is peaceful. He wears the diadem, earrings and the rest of the "thirteen peaceful
ornaments."[4] His upper garment is made from multicolored silks; his
lower is red. He sits with legs crossed in the vajra position.[5] His body, endowed with the [thirty-two] major and [eighty] minor marks of physical perfection,[6] shines with a lustrous glow as he meditates with a joyful
heart.

On the crown of his head, seated one above the other in a vertical
column [starting with the first named and going upward], are [the
gurus of the Mahamudra lineage]: Padma Nyinjay Wongpo, Mipham
Chodrub Gyatso, Dudul Dorje, Chokyi Jungnay, Jongchub Dorje, Chokyi
Dondrub, Yeshe Dorje, Yeshe Nyingpo, Choying Dorje, Chokyi Wong-
chug, Wongchug Dorje, Konchog Yanlag, Michod Dorje, Songyay
Nyanpa, Chodrag Gyatso, Paljor Dondrub, Jampal Zangpo, Tongwa
Dondan, Rigpay Raldri, Deshin Shegpa, Khachod Wongpo, Rolpay
Dorje, Yungton Dorjepal, Rongjung Dorje, Orgyanpa Rinchenpal,
Drubchen Pakshi, Pomdrag Sonam Dorje, Drogon Rechen Songyaydrag,
Dusum Khyenpa, Nyam-me Dagpo, Jetsun Mila, Marpa Lotsa, Maitripa,
Shawari, Phapa Ludrub, Saraha, and Lodro Rinchen.[7]

In the sky surrounding [the column of gurus] sit the Six Ornaments of Jambudvipa,[8] Tilopa, Naropa and the learned and spiritually

accomplished gurus of Drikhung, Drugpa, Tshalpa and Talung.[9] These
and the other gurus of India and Tibet appear like a cluster of clouds.

YIDAMS[10]

On the eastern branch, standing on lotuses, each topped by a solar
disc on which lies a corpse, are Vajravarahi (Dorje Phamo) with Cakra-
samvara (Khorlo Demchog), Hevajra (Kye Dorje) and Guhyasamaja
(Songwa Dupa); Mahamaya (Gyuma chenpo), Vajrakapalin (Songyay
Todpa), and Catur-Vajrasana (Dorje Danshi); Kala-ari (Dranag),
Shanmukha (Dongdrug), and Vajrabhairava (Dorje Jigjay); Kalacakra
(Du-kyi khorlo) and the rest of the yidams of the four or six tantras,
surrounded by hosts of [attendant] deities.

BUDDHAS

On the right hand branch, seated on a lotus and moon seat atop a
lion throne, is our teacher, Shakyamuni, surrounded by the thousand
Buddhas of the fortunate kalpas[11] and all the other Buddhas of the three
times and the ten directions.[12]

DHARMA

On the rear branch are the twelve divisions of the Buddha's
Dharma-teachings, particularly the Mahayana and the secret Mantrayana.
The various books, whose ends face you, are [wrapped in fine cloth]
of all colors of the rainbow. They have golden title-flaps.[13] The vowels
and consonants [which comprise the written words] murmur aloud [of
their own accord].

SANGHA

On the left-hand branch sit the countless Bodhisattvas, Shravakas,
and Pratyekabuddhas of the Mahayana and Hinayana Sangha. They include the Lords of the Three Families and the rest of Buddha's Eight
Sons, Bodhisattvas of fortunate kalpas, the Buddha's Excellent Pair of
disciples, Ananda, the Sixteen Elders and others.[14]

DHARMAPALAS, DAKAS, DAKINIS[15]

Beneath the refuge tree are inconceivable numbers of "awareness deities," including dharmapalas, dakas and dakinis. The principal ones are Mahakala (Dorje Berchan), [flanked by] Svayambhurajni-Shridevi (Rongjungma Palden Lhamo) and the four and six-armed Mahakala.

Visualize yourself standing on the ground, facing all these sources of refuge. Your father and mother, most important of all the limitless sentient beings who now surround you, stand at your right and left [respectively]. [The crowd of sentient beings includes] in particular, hated enemies, obscuring demons and various demonic beings who from time without beginning have been bent on revenge against you. With you as their leader, the whole crowd of beings which you have assembled now venerates physically, verbally and mentally the sources of refuge. Each one joins his palms in prayer, [performs prostrations], engenders faith and devotion, and recites the refuge vow a hundred or a thousand times or more.[16]

[As you recite the words], think about what they mean, and do not let your mind stray from an attitude of reverence.

Then engender the aspiration [to reach enlightenment for the sake of all beings by reciting the Bodhisattva vow[17] three times].

[Then, recite the prayers of rejoicing].[18]

[Now, pray for universal engenderment of bodhicitta],[19] and for the success of all Bodhisattvas' deeds.[20]

[Recite the prayer for the Four Immeasurables three times].[21]

The sources of refuge, the throne and the rest dissolve into light and are absorbed into yourself. Think that your own body, speech and mind have become inseparable from the body, speech and mind of your root-guru as Vajradhara.[22] Let your mind rest naturally.

[Recite the prayer for] dedicating merit.[23]

COMMENTARY

The following points should be understood in relation to Taking Refuge: In this world, we naturally seek someone capable of protecting us or providing refuge from causes of fear and anxiety, such as severe illness, and so on. Preoccupied by the countless fears which plague us throughout this life, future lives and in the bardo, we could sink forever in the ocean of samsaric suffering. Neither our father, mother, relatives, friends, powerful gods, nagas, nor similar beings are capable of giving us refuge from samsaric suffering. Nor are we ourselves capable of driving it off. If we do not find some [effective source of refuge], we will be utterly helpless.

Only the Precious Ones have the ability to rescue us from samsara. Only those who can save themselves will be able to save others.

THE SIX SOURCES OF REFUGE

[The six sources of refuge consist of the Three Jewels and the Three Roots]. The Three Jewels are the Buddha, Dharma and Sangha, to which the Mantrayana adds the Three Roots:

1. The guru is the root of all blessing.[24]
2. The yidam is the root of all *siddhi*.[25]
3. The dakinis and dharmapalas are the root of all Buddha-activity.[26]

These Three Roots are included in the Three Jewels. The Mantrayana holds that all six are encompassed by the root-guru alone.

Furthermore, Buddha [manifests in the three following ways]: the Dharmakaya, which knows all things, both as they are and as they appear; the Sambhogakaya, possessed of the "five certainties"; and the Nirmanakaya, which takes the form of [any type of worldly] art or skill, of a being [who is an incarnation of an enlightened one], or of a Buddha. "Buddha" thus includes the three *kayas*.[27]

"Dharma" refers to the scriptural Dharma:[28] the words, sentences and letters in the Buddha's verbal teachings and the recited [prayers and mantras].

"Dharma" also includes the realization-Dharma:[29] the ground, Dharmadhatu, *tathata;* the Noble Truth of the Cessation of Suffering which is the result; and the Noble Truth of the Path—all of which lead to enlightenment. "Dharma" thus includes both scripture and realization.

"Sangha" includes the real Sangha,[30] comprised of Bodhisattvas who will not regress, and the provisional Sangha,[31] comprised of Shravakas, Pratyekabuddhas and Arhats.

Since Buddha has demonstrated what should be accepted and what should be rejected, regard Buddha as your teacher. Since his teachings are the basis for practice, regard the Dharma as the path. Since this path is unfamiliar to you, you will need the constant instructions and example of the holy ones. Thus, seek companions in the Sangha.

When you reach the goal, your awareness will be the same as the enlightened awareness of all Buddhas. You will no longer need the Dharma and Sangha. The ultimate refuge is Buddha alone.

In these times of philosophical speculation, there is much discussion on how [the sources of refuge] should be regarded and on what is or is not a source of refuge. One who is simply practicing [Taking Refuge] and establishing wholesome habits has no need of such [speculation]. He simply needs to develop faith and devotion.

Certain factors will promote the awakening of faith. In the sutras, that which is termed the "Buddha to be placed before you," such as an image, stupa, etc., is a symbol of the Buddha. By implication, a volume of the sutras or tantras [is a symbol of] the holy Dharma, and a member of the practicing Buddhist community [is a symbol of the Sangha.]. If you meditate that these [symbols] are the real Precious Ones, you will take refuge with faith and devotion.

Taking Refuge in the Hinayana or worldly manner[32] is improper and will not do you much good. It is extremely important that you think: "I take refuge from this day until all sentient beings, immeasurable as the sky, have reached enlightenment." Through this [thought, your practice] becomes the Mahayana refuge.

FOUR SPECIAL CONDITIONS FOR TAKING REFUGE

1. Having learned the basics of the proper way to think about the Precious Ones, appreciate their qualities.

2. Appreciate the Buddha, Dharma and Sangha's superiority to non-Buddhist teachers, false paths and heretics.

3. Based on this appreciation, make a sincere commitment to always take refuge.

4. Even if your life is at stake, do not take refuge in anyone but the Precious Ones.

It is said that to take refuge under these four special conditions is to take refuge properly.

It is not enough to repeat [after the guru] the words, "I take refuge." You must also have the deepest confidence in the Precious Ones. If you have this kind of confidence, you will never lack the protection of their compassion.

While you experience the unavoidable effects of the bad deeds which ripen in this life, you may feel that the Precious Ones' compassion has been vanquished. But if you have deep confidence in them, they will certainly protect you in all future lives.

If, when experiencing some slight unpleasantness, you say "The Precious Ones have no compassion!" or you expect to be helped by such means as divination, exorcism or medical treatment—these are signs of stupidity.

If their compassion has not emerged in your life, it is not because they have no blessing to confer. You yourself are to blame for failing to pray for it!

Therefore, continually think of the Precious Ones' qualities, meditate with faith and pray intently. Do not accumulate bad deeds by talking nonsense or slandering others. Pay homage to symbols[33] of [Buddha's] body, speech and mind, as well as to people who wear the yellow [monastic] robes with faith and devotion, conceiving of them as the real Precious Ones. Restore old images and make new ones. Do not lay them on bare ground or in a place where they may be disturbed. It is unthinkable to trade an image for food or pawn it for cash. It is wrong to walk on even a scrap of tsa-tsa[34] or a single letter.

Remembering [the Precious Ones'] kindness, offer homage, praise and other devotions with your body, speech and mind.

Remembering their compassion, encourage others to take refuge and tell them about the Precious Ones' great qualities.

Remembering the benefits of doing so, repeat the refuge meditation six times in the course of each day and night.

Remembering the shortcomings of samsara, never reject the sources of refuge, even if your life is at stake.

No matter what comes your way—happiness, misery, prominence or degradation—think only of the Precious Ones with profound confidence. Do not become discouraged.

In brief, once you have taken refuge in the Buddha, (1.) do not rely on worldly gods. Once you have taken refuge in the Dharma, (2.) reject thoughts and deeds injurious to sentient beings. Once you have taken refuge in the Sangha, (3.) do not associate with heretics or their sympathizers.[35]

Done properly, Taking Refuge includes most of the practices in the gradual paths to enlightenment of the Sutra- and the Mantrayana. But if you merely "act it out" without becoming deeply involved, even if you talk about "emptiness" in lofty language, you have strayed from the path into a deep chasm.

RESULTS OF TAKING REFUGE

If you practice Taking Refuge continuously and it never leaves your thoughts, you become a Buddhist. Your minor wrong-doings are purified; your major ones decrease. Human and non-human obstacles cannot affect you. Your vows, studies and other wholesome activities become more and more fruitful. If you truly rely on the Precious Ones, you will not be born in the lower realms even if you feel yourself being pushed in that direction.

According to the *Saddharmapundarika sutra*:[36]

"Even lay disciples and counterfeit monks[37] who embrace my teaching will totally pass beyond sorrow within this very kalpa. Not one will be left behind!"

Thus, we have touched upon the considerations which accompany Taking Refuge, and the great benefits to be gained from practicing it.

ENGENDERING THE ENLIGHTENED ATTITUDE

Engendering the Enlightened Attitude (*bodhicitta*) accompanies Taking Refuge.

Generally speaking, once an individual's thoughts have turned to the Dharma, he will travel the Dharma-path only if he develops the enlightened attitude. If he does not develop it, he will not travel the Dharma-path. Whether his wholesome acts have been many or few, once he has acquired the means for attaining Buddhahood,[38] he is said to have started on the Dharma-path.

How could we possibly measure the merit accumulated by wholesome acts undertaken in an enlightened attitude? Even commonplace acts become means for attaining Buddhahood [when accompanied by the enlightened attitude]. Thus, a sutra says:

"If you desire complete perfect Buddhahood, you need not be trained in many aspects of the Dharma, but only in one. Which one? The enlightened attitude!"

THE TWO TYPES OF BODHICITTA

There are two types of bodhicitta: the relative and the ultimate. Since these are the basis of the "eighty-four thousand Dharma teachings,"[39] it is difficult to give a condensed explanation. At this time, when you are immersed in meditating, you have no need for the many teachings on the two types of bodhicitta. But if you wish to know about them, study the six standard reference works of the Kadampa sect,[40] and other texts.

In brief, relative bodhicitta is essentially compassion. Ultimate bodhicitta is essentially insight. Development of the second type depends on the first. Phadampa[41] said, "A fish will take to water but not to dry land; realization will not arise in the absence of compassion." Just so, ultimate bodhicitta, realization of the undistorted true nature of things, depends on relative bodhicitta. A person who has not yet realized [the ultimate nature of things] but has awakened the force of genuine compassion will be quite capable of working physically, verbally and mentally for the welfare of others.

ENGENDERING RELATIVE BODHICITTA: THE BODHISATTVA VOW

Since the presence or absence of the relative type is the sole determinant for the presence or absence of bodhicitta *per se*, a means of engendering it must first be found. Specific practices must be employed to engender its "aspiration" and "perseverance" aspects.

A superior type of person engenders it by simply reciting the Bodhisattva vow three times with sincerity and understanding, while facing any symbol [of the Three Jewels].[42]

Ordinary people should receive the vow from a spiritual teacher belonging to an unbroken [lineage of transmission of this vow].

Then, it is best to recite the vow six times during the day and six times at night; second best to recite it at the beginning and end of each of the four watches of the day; and acceptable to recite it once during the day and once during the night.

ASPIRATION- AND PERSEVERANCE-BODHICITTA

To engender aspiration-bodhicitta is to constantly think, "I will attain omniscient Buddhahood for the sake of all sentient beings." Aspiration is like desiring to go somewhere.

To engender perseverance-bodhicitta is to perform wholesome acts which will actualize that promise, while thinking, "To that end, I will apply the instructions for Sahaja Mahamudra meditation."[43] Perseverance is like actually starting out on a path.

[In the refuge practice,][44] before you dissolve the sources of refuge, you recite the Bodhisattva vow three times. Thus, before that excellent gathering, you engender aspiration-bodhicitta just as the Buddhas and Bodhisattvas of the past have done. Then you engender perseverance-bodhicitta by thinking, "Just as they did, so must I engender bodhicitta and train myself in each stage of the Six Perfections[45] for the sake of my parents—all sentient beings."

Then, you joyfully meditate that you have engendered the enlightened attitude [and recite the prayers of rejoicing].

Then, you think that others praise your achievement, and you pray [for universal engenderment of bodhicitta and for the Four Immeasurables].

Then, you dissolve the sources of refuge into yourself.

You repeatedly renew your Bodhisattva vow by reciting it while thinking that the lion-throne, with the lotus and moon upon it, and the teacher Shakyamuni surrounded by the Sangha composed of the Eight Sons, Sixteen Elders, Bodhisattvas, Shravakas and Pratyekabuddhas are actually present in the sky before you.

Finally, you rest in non-conceptualization.

TRAINING IN ASPIRATION-BODHICITTA

Keeping the Bodhisattva Vow

The training in engendering bodhicitta is very broad, since it is comprised of all religious acts and practices. But briefly, training in aspiration-bodhicitta entails [keeping the Bodhisattva vow].

Since (1.) mentally abandoning sentient beings and (2.) adopting attitudes contrary to bodhicitta will uproot and destroy the Bodhisattva vow, it is crucial that you reject both of these once you have taken the vow.

Regardless of the number of sentient beings involved, harboring malicious thoughts, such as "Even if I have a chance to help you, I won't!" or being filled with hate, envy or anger toward others is the transgression called "mentally abandoning sentient beings."

Likewise, thinking "I can't do anything to help myself or others! I may as well become a common worldly man! Complete Buddhahood is so hard to attain that it doesn't matter if I engender bodhicitta or not! I can't possibly help anyone!"; adopting the attitude of a Shravaka or Pratyekabuddha, who is merely concerned with his own welfare; thinking "The benefits of bodhicitta are not that great"; or relaxing the vow— all these are attitudes contrary to bodhicitta.

If you do not correct these attitudes within three hours, the vow is broken.[46] Always be wary of them! Even if they arise unconsciously, immediate Confession[47] will repair the vow.

In brief, never let the excellent attitude—the desire to establish even enemies and harmful demons in Buddhahood—deteriorate. Even offenses as serious as a Shravaka's worst misdeeds[48] cannot destroy bodhicitta. Thus, carry out all the truly beneficial acts you can. Even if you are incapable of [actually helping others], always maintain the intention to help them in the future.

Remembering the Enlightened Attitude

Reject the "four black deeds" which will cause you to forget the enlightened attitude in all your future existences. Cultivate the "four white deeds" which will cause you to remember it in all your future existences.

The first black deed is to consciously lie in order to deceive a guru or other worshipful person. Whether you fool him or not, whether your words are many or few, it is wrong to slander and lie, even as a joke.

[The first white deed is to tell the truth under all circumstances].

The second black deed is to cause others to regret their wholesome acts. You ought to cause others to regret their harmful acts, but [wholesome acts] are no grounds for regret. You will be at fault whether or not you succeed in causing them to regret [their wholesome acts].

The second white deed is to do all you can to urge all beings to follow the three yanas[49] (especially the Mahayana), and perform wholesome action. Induce them to pray for supreme enlightenment.

The third black deed is to publicly or privately use a single word of censure against any sentient being who has even verbally engendered bodhicitta. [This is because by engendering bodhicitta] he has joined the Bodhisattvas.

The third white deed is to praise rather than condemn even ordinary sentient beings. Since all sentient beings possess the "heart of Buddha," and are the field for your acquisition of the Accumulations and removal of obscurations, it has been declared that they do not differ from Buddhas.

The fourth black deed is to physically, mentally or verbally cheat, deceive or double-cross anyone to further your own interests.

The fourth white deed is to make others' welfare your personal concern by wishing to establish all sentient beings in a blessed and happy state during their present and future lives. You should always speak sincerely, like a father to his son.

Briefly, everything [you must do to engender aspiration-bodhicitta] is encompassed by the statements: Give all profit and victory to others; accept all loss and defeat for yourself.

Since it is the Bodhisattva vow's intention which is most important,

try to keep bodhicitta continually in mind, in all you do or say. Since
increasing the Two Accumulations leads to the steady growth of bodhicitta, train yourself to do this.

1. Carrying Out the Bodhisattva's Ten Tasks

From the *Sagaramatipariprccha sutra*:[50]

A Bodhisattva is said to have ten tasks. They are: 1. To abide in faith,
which is the root, and rely on a spiritual teacher; 2. to energetically study
all aspects of the holy Dharma; 3. to energetically perform wholesome acts,
impelled by the earnest desire [to help others], and to never abandon [this
task]; 4. to carefully avoid any wasteful acts; 5. to help sentient beings to
spiritual maturity, without attachment to the merit one accumulates by so
doing; 6. to adhere to the holy Dharma without concern for life and limb;
7. to never be satisfied with the amount of merit one has accumulated; 8. to
assiduously accumulate transcending awareness; 9. to always remember the
highest goal, and 10. to pursue one's chosen path with skillful means.

Carry out these tasks assiduously! As for the training in perseverance: just as a farmer who wants a good harvest must not simply seed
his crops but cultivate them as well, you who want to attain Buddhahood
need more than aspiration. You must also perform all types of Bodhi-
sattva-activity to the best of your ability.

2. Practicing the Six Perfections

1. Give gifts; 2. observe moral conduct; 3. practice patience; 4.
apply strenuousness; 5. cultivate meditative concentration; 6. cultivate
insight. Practice these Six Perfections!

In brief, "There is nothing in [the Six Perfections] that the Buddha
and his sons[51] have not practiced," so perform all types of wholesome
acts and joyfully contemplate those performed by others.

3. Applying the Four Immeasurables

To apply the Four Immeasurables is to think of all sentient beings,
immeasurable as the sky, without distinguishing between "enemy,"
"friend," or "neutral," with these [four attitudes]:

1. Benevolence: the desire to establish all sentient beings in a state of happiness which they have not previously enjoyed and to establish them in the cause of happiness, wholesome action.

2. Compassion: the desire to free them from suffering from this day forward and to remove the cause of their suffering, unwholesome action.

3. [Sympathetic] joy: delight in the physical and mental happiness of others.

4. Equanimity: the attitude that of all sentient beings, who are like your mother, not one is more or less important than another. No attachment is felt toward one or aversion toward another, near or far. All are regarded equally.

These are the Four Immeasurables.

Once you have begun Mahayana practice, applying [the Four Immeasurables,] the essence of the Dharma, should become your principal concern.

According to the Kadampas' instructions, thinking about the connections between certain causes and results leads an individual to develop benevolence and the rest. Think:

"I must attain Buddhahood above all else.

I must engender the enlightened attitude, the cause [of attaining Buddhahood].

Compassion is the cause of [engendering the enlightened attitude].

Benevolence is the cause of compassion.

Remembering past kindness is the cause [of benevolence].

Appreciation of the fact that all sentient beings have been my parents is the cause of [remembering kindness].

I must appreciate this!

Having done so, I must first remember my present mother's kindness and meditate on benevolence. Then I must broaden this attitude to include all sentient beings who live and breathe!"

The two "roots of degeneracy" are: 1. To pretend to be a Bodhisattva while hoping to be seen as a "good Buddhist," hoping to obtain food, clothing or fame, or hoping to appear better than others. 2. To act hypocritically, and call yourself a "realized being" or siddha. Apply the antidote: meditate on the rarity of the opportunities and blessings [of a human existence] and on impermanence.

To perform a few wholesome acts or religious practices merely because you desire godly or human happiness in future lives is contrary to

bodhicitta. [Apply the antidote]: think about action and result, and
samsara's shortcomings.

To think only of your own welfare instead of the welfare of others
is to ignore the essential. [Apply the antidote]: meditate on exchanging
your own [wholesome acts and happiness] for the [unwholesome acts
and suffering] of others.[52] This is most important.

Moreover, [remember that] all sentient beings are the same as you,
for they want to be happy and do not want to suffer. Like yourself, they
lack any real nature of their own.

Since you are but one, and sentient beings are many, they are not
merely equal but are much more important than yourself. Therefore,
do not simply play with the idea, but be confident and determined in
your intention to establish all beings in Buddhahood once you yourself
have attained it.

To do this profitably, do not cherish yourself, but regard any sentient
being as much more important than yourself. You must be prepared to
undergo severe suffering to bring happiness to others and eagerly think
and act solely for their benefit.

Nowadays, even if we perform a few wholesome acts, most of us
do it for our own sake. Carrying out your appointed task only for your
own sake will not get you anywhere!

You must move, walk, sleep and sit—to say nothing of practicing
religion—with the sole intention of helping others!

4. Sending and Receiving

When you are beset by illness or demons, tormented by gossip or
by an upsurge of conflicting emotions, take on the misfortunes of all
other sentient beings. Knowing that your former deeds are the cause [of
present sorrow], do not be depressed when sorrow strikes, but take up
the sorrows of others.

When you are happy, use your wealth, influence and merit to perform wholesome acts. Do not sit idly by, but engage your body and
speech in wholesome acts such as praying for the happiness of all sentient beings.

In brief, do not let any of your acts become entangled in self-
interest, but assess your Dharma practice by the extent to which it has
abolished ego-clinging.

As you inhale through your nose, take in the black mass of all the
misery, harmful acts and obscurations of all sentient beings, and let it

melt into your heart. As you exhale through your nose, send out the "white rays" of all the merit and happiness you have accumulated through beginningless time. Think that when all sentient beings have received it, they will attain Buddhahood. Joyously meditate, and continuously recite:

> *When I am happy, may my merit flow to others!*
> *May its blessing fill the sky!*
> *When I am unhappy, may the sorrows of all beings be mine.*
> *May the ocean of suffering run dry!*

Even on your deathbed when you cannot perform any other practice, use your time Sending and Receiving for as long as you can breathe.

When subject to misfortunes such as illness, mental disturbance, disputes or lawsuits, do not blame others. Blame yourself, thinking that it is simply due to your own ego-clinging.

Since [all sentient beings]—your enemies, friends, and those in between—provide you with a basis for the mental discipline [of Sending and Receiving] and help you to get rid of harmful acts and obscurations, think how very kind they are.

Do not say or do anything simply because you want others to think that you are free of ego-clinging. All your acts must be pure as the *vinaya*.

Do not discuss the faults of others. Realize that their "faults" are actually your own impure projections. Do not call attention to human failings, use abusive language or fierce mantras against non-humans[53] or other creatures. Do not relegate troublesome tasks to others or have them do your dirty-work.

It is wrong to enjoy the prospect of an opponent's defeat, to be glad when an enemy dies and contemplate profit from a competitor's illness. Without concern for the state of your health or your capacity to reply to gossip, meditate on the enlightened attitude. Intently meditate on [engendering compassion for] difficult objects of compassion, such as enemies and obstructive creatures.

Regularize sporadic Dharma practice caused by uncertainty about the Dharma. Since it is to your own advantage to practice Dharma, do not boast about the hardships you are undergoing.

When others harm you by calling attention to your faults, by humiliating, beating or flaring up at you, do not respond but simply meditate with compassion.

Never display your happy or unhappy moods.

If you will not endure any self-sacrifice or give others any help, you have missed the significance of Engendering the Enlightened Attitude. Exchanging your [wholesome acts and happiness] for [the unwholesome acts and suffering of] others is an especially forceful type of skillful means, so apply it with great determination.

RESULTS OF ENGENDERING THE ENLIGHTENED ATTITUDE

Merely Engendering the Enlightened Attitude purifies countless harmful acts and immeasurably enlarges wholesome ones. The merit you acquire in one instant of bodhicitta exceeds [the merit you would acquire by] offering each of the Buddhas as many vast realms filled to the brim with precious gems as there are grains of sand in the Ganges! We need not mention its measureless blessing! It is the heart of the entire Dharma.

SUBSEQUENT ACTION: THE TWO TYPES OF MORAL CONDUCT BEFITTING A BODHISATTVA

Since all Bodhisattva-activities, such as the Six Perfections, arise from compassion alone, do not say "I have meditated for this many months" or "How pitiful is this one suffering sentient being." Cultivate constant, pervasive, great compassion for all beings, free of bias or partiality. [Cultivate the two types of moral conduct]:

1. Cultivate all types of wholesome action for the sake of your own spiritual development. This is the "moral conduct of collecting wholesome dharmas."

2. Convince other sentient beings to perform all appropriate wholesome acts for the sake of their spiritual development. This is the "moral conduct which benefits others."

Your Bodhisattva vow covers everything that falls within the two types of moral conduct, so it is proper to practice them both. It is said that for a Bodhisattva not to do so is a failing. Thus, whatever happens, engage in wholesome activity and encourage others to do the same.

Anyone who feels it is sufficient to apply just one [type of moral conduct], is simply clinging to an insubstantial meditative experience which will not withstand adverse circumstances.[54] Such behavior stems from ignorance of the Buddha's words and the spiritual biographies of holy men.

NOTES

1. See *'Phags-lam,* 107/5–108/3. This section of the liturgy describes the visualization.

2. Each item is the finest of its kind; e.g., the water is cool, sweet, gentle, clear, free of impurities, soothes the stomach and clears the throat. In ancient Indian thought the wish-fulfilling tree, which bears any desired fruit, symbolizes worldly power (see chap. 4, n. 24). Here, reliance on the sources of refuge visualized in this tree will yield man's highest desire, attainment of Buddhahood.

3. The vajra (Tib. *rdorje*) and bell held with the hands crossed in front of the heart, symbolize the integration of insight (the vajra) and compassion (the bell).

4. The eight pieces of jewelry and five silken garments worn by Buddhas and Bodhisattvas generally symbolize the enriching, enlivening influence of the Sambhogakaya.

5. Full lotus position.

6. Traditional physical appearance of a Buddha, including long earlobes, webbed fingers and so on.

7. These gurus comprise the Mahamudra lineage up to the time of Jamgon Kongtrul. We have updated the list below, by adding the six names of the most recent members of that lineage.

   1. Norbu Dondrub (Nor-bu Don-grub, ca. 1870): disciple of Jamgon Kongtrul. He was Kalu Rinpoche's root-guru and also a teacher of the sixteenth Karmapa, Rongjung rigpay Dorje (Rang-byung rig-pa'i rDorje, b. 1924). According to Kalu Rinpoche, when Lama Norbu died his body dissolved into a magnificent rainbow in the sky.

   2. Jamgon Khyentse Odzer ('Jam-mgon mKhyen-brtse 'Od-zer, b. 1899): second incarnation of Jamgon Kongtrul.

   3. Padma Wongchog (Padma dBang-mchog rGyal-po, 1854-?): the tenth Situ Rinpoche.

   4. Khakhyab Dorje (mKha'-khyab rDorje, 1845-1924): the fifteenth Karmapa.

   5. Yontan Gyatso (Ngag-dbang Yon-tan rGya-mtsho, also known as Jamgon Kongtrul, 1813-99): the name given to Kongtrul upon his ordination as a Karma Kagyud monk in 1833. It is the name with which he signs this text.

   6. Tegchog Dorje (Theg-mchog rDorje, 1797-1845), the fourteenth Karmapa.

   7. Padma Nyinjay Wongpo (Padma Nyin-byed, 1774-1853): the ninth Situ Rinpoche and Kongtrul's root-guru.

   8. Mipham Chodrub Gyatso (Mi-pham Chos-grub rGya-mtsho, ca. 1750): the tenth Shamar (Zhwa-dmar: "red hat") tulku, the line whose source is the Buddha Amitabha.

7. (*Cont.*)
    9. Dudul Dorje (bDud-'dul rDorje, 1733-97): the thirteenth
Karmapa.
    10. Chokyi Jungnay (Situ Chos-kyi 'byung-gnas, also known as
bsTan-pa'i Nyin-byed, 1700-75): the eighth Situ Rinpoche. He
founded Palpung monastery in 1727.
    11. Jongchub Dorje (Byang-chub rDorje, 1703-32): the twelfth
Karmapa.
    12. Chokyi Dondrub (dPal-chen Chos-kyi don-grub, also known
as rNam-rol mchog-pa, 1695-1732): the eighth Shamar tulku, or
Shamarpa.
    13. Yeshe Dorje (Ye-shes rDorje, 1675-1702): the eleventh
Karmapa.
    14. Yeshe Nyingpo (Ye-shes sNying-po, also known as Padma
Gar-gi dbang-phyug, 1639-94): the seventh Shamarpa.
    15. Choying Dorje (Chos-dbyings rDorje, 1604-74): the tenth
Karmapa.
    16. Chokyi Wongchug (Chos-kyi dbang-phyug, 1584-1635): the
sixth Shamarpa.
    17. Wongchug Dorje (dBang-phyug rDorje, 1556-1603): the
ninth Karmapa, principal author of *'Phags-lam bgrod-pa'i shing-rta,*
the liturgy for these practices.
    18. Konchog Yanlag (dKon-mchog Yan-lag, 1525-83): the fifth
Shamarpa.
    19. Michod Dorje (Mi-bskyod rDorje, also known as Chos-
grags dPal-bzang, 1507-54): the eighth Karmapa.
    20. Songyay Nyanpa (Sangs-rgyas mNyen-pa, also known as
bKra-shis dPal-'byor, ca. 1450): the fourth Situ, teacher of Michod
Dorje and pupil of the fourth Shamar Rinpoche.
    21. Chodrag Gyatso (Chos-grags rGya-mtsho, 1454-1506): the
seventh Karmapa.
    22. Paljor Dondrub (dPal-'byor Don-grub, ca. 1400): first
Gyaltshab Rinpoche and a close disciple of the sixth Karmapa.
    23. Jampal Zangpo ('Jam-dpal bZang-po, ca. 1400): an eminent
Karma Kagyud guru.
    24. Tongwa Dondan (mThong-ba Don-ldan, 1416-53): the
sixth Karmapa.
    25. Rigpay Raldri (Rig-pa'i ral-gri, also known as Ratnabhadra,
ca. 1400): a Mahamudra teacher.
    26. Deshin Shegpa (De-bzhin gshegs-pa, 1384-1415): the fifth
Karmapa, famous for the magical feats by which he dissuaded the
Yung-lo Emperor from invading Tibet. The same Emperor presented
to Deshin Shegpa the black hat which became the Karmapas' trade-
mark.
    27. Khachod Wongpo (mKha'-spyod dBang-po, 1350-1405):
the second Shamar Rinpoche.
    28. Rolpay Dorje (Rol-pa'i rDorje, 1340-83): the fourth Kar-

7. *(Cont.)*
mapa, known for his magic powers and as a teacher of the Gelugpa founder Tsongkhapa.

29. Yungton Dorjepal (gYung-ston rDorje-dpal, also known as gYung-ston-pa, 1283-?) : a Mahamudra teacher.

30. Rongjung Dorje (Rang-byung rDorje, 1284-1339) : the third Karmapa.

31. Orgyanpa Rinchenpal (Orgyan-pa Rin-chen-dpal, also known as rGod-tsang-pa or mGon-po rDorje, 1229-1309 or 1189-1258) : founder of the Tod (sTod) branch of the Drugpa ('Brug-pa) Kagyud sect.

32. Drubchen Pakshi (Grub-chen Pagshi or Karma Pakshi, 1206-83) : the second Karmapa, first of that line to visit China, where he stunned the Taoists with skill in magic and debate.

33. Pomdrag Sonam Dorje (sPom-brag bSod-nams rDorje, also known as sPom-brag-pa, ca. 1100) : a Mahamudra master.

34. Drogon Rechen Songyaydrag ('Gro-mgon Ras-chen Sangs-rgyas grags, ca. 1100) : the first Situ Rinpoche.

35. Dusum Khyenpa (Dus-gsum mkhyen-pa, 1110-93) : the first Karmapa. See H. E. Richardson, "The Karma-pa Sect," *JRAS*, 1958: 139–64.

36. Nyam-me Dagpo (mNyam-med Dwags-po, also known as sGam-po-pa, 1079-1153) : the renowned Kagyudpa author and teacher.

37. Jetsun Mila (rJe-btsun Mila, or Milarepa, 1052-1135) : the great yogin.

38. Marpa Lotsa (Mar-pa Lo-tsa-wa, also known as Lho-brag-pa, 1012-96) : Marpa the translator, Mila's guru.

39. Maitripa (ca. 1150) : an Indian teacher of both Atisha and Marpa.

40. Shawari (Shavaripa, ca. 657) : an Indian mahasiddha, said to have instituted the cult of Vajrayogini, so important to the Kagyud sect. See T. Schmid, *The Eighty-Five Siddhas*. Stockholm: Reports from the Scientific Expedition to the Northwestern Provinces of China, pt. 8, vol. 7, p. 60 and pl. 5.

41. Phapa Ludrub ('Phags-pa kLu-grub or kLu-grub sNying-po, 645 A.D.?) : another Indian mahasiddha. See Schmid, *Siddhas*, pp. 20–27.

42. Saraha (ca. 633 A.D.) : the Indian mahasiddha renowned for his *dohas* or tantric songs. See H. V. Guenther, *Royal Song of Saraha*. Seattle: Univ. of Wash., 1969.

43. Lodro Rinchen (bLo-gros Rin-chen, dates unknown) : an Indian siddha directly inspired by Vajradhara. (Lama)
The source of this lineage is, of course, Vajradhara.

8. Six great Indian teachers: Aryadeva, Asanga, Vasumitra, Dignaga, Dharmakirti and Nagendra.

9. Four Kagyudpa subsects.

10. Tutelary or meditational deities. Generally, a yidam represents Buddha as seen by an ordinary being at some particular stage of his spiritual development, thus serving as a means to approach that remote goal. An aspirant acquires a yidam by receiving that deity's empowerment, practicing his meditation, reciting his mantra and praying to him. Each aspirant specializes in the group of practices associated with one particular yidam whom he chooses with his guru's help, to suit his own needs and disposition.

The question of yidams and their functions is a complex one. The groupings of yidams as well as the particular siddhi associated with each one vary from text to text. But generally speaking, meditating on the yidams below, as well as other key deities, clears away obscurations. This leads to the ability to practice various yogas by which one's ordinary life, tainted by the five poisons (pride, desire and attachment, aversion, jealousy and bewilderment) is transformed into enlightened existence possessed of the five transcending awarenesses (transcending awareness as the Dharmadhatu, as mirror-like clarity, as evenness, as discrimination and as accomplishment). (Lama)

Vajravarahi and Cakrasamvara (rDorje Phag-mo and 'Khor-lo bDe-mchog) are the chief female and male yidams of the Kagyudpa sect.

11. A fortunate kalpa is any era in which a Buddha appears. (Lama)

12. "Three times": past, present, and future. "Ten directions": north, south, west, east, the "four corners" and the zenith and nadir of the traditional Buddhist universe. (LPL)

13. gdong-khra: rectangular cloth, bearing the title, which is draped over the end of a Tibetan-style book. Books are stacked with this end facing front, for easy identification.

14. "Lords of the Three Families": Manjushri (Bodhisattva of insight), Vajrapani (Bodhisattva of spiritual attainment) and Avalokiteshvara (Bodhisattva of compassion).

The rest of the "Eight Sons" or chief Bodhisattvas are Kshitigarbha, Sarvanivaranavishkambhi, Akashagarbha, Maitreya and Samantabhadra.

The "Excellent Pair" were Shakyamuni's chief disciples, Shariputra and Maudgalyayana.

Ananda was Buddha's personal attendant.

The "Sixteen Elders" were disciples of Shakyamuni who preached the Dharma in various lands after the Buddha's death.

15. All three are termed "awareness deities" (ye-shes-kyi lha) because they personify certain aspects of enlightened beings. For example, the six-armed Mahakala personifies the wrathful aspect of Avalokiteshvara, the Bodhisattva of compassion.

Dharmapalas help clear away obstacles to the aspirant's practice, and thus often appear threatening until these have been overcome. As with the yidam, the aspirant and his guru choose the dharmapala who best suits his needs, and he receives the empowerment and practices the deity's rituals.

Dorje Berchan (rDorje Ber-can) or Ber-nag-che is the main Kagyudpa dharmapala, a form of Mahakala.

These enlightened dharmapalas are thus distinguished from the "worldly deities" ('jig-rten-pa'i lha), samsaric demons who are not sources of refuge.

Dakas (male) and dakinis (female) share some of the dharmapalas' functions. Dakinis or yoginis are female Bodhisattvas who sometimes act as messengers between ordinary beings and enlightened ones. See R. Nebesky-Wojkowitz, *Oracles and Demons of Tibet.* S'Gravenhage: Mouton, 1956, particularly pp. 3–202.

16. See *'Phags-lam*, 108/3–6. The refuge vow, a verbal commitment to the six sources of refuge and the goal which they personify, is recited while performing full prostrations. Since the recitations take longer than prostrations and both must be performed a total of 111,111 times, the missing recitations may be added either after completing all the prostrations or after each session of prostrations. (Lama)

The particular refuge vow which appears in *'Phags-lam* is the most elaborate of several Tibetan versions. Earlier Indian versions invoked only the Buddha, Dharma and Sangha. The guru may have been added by the Tibetans. The invocation of the other three sources identifies this as a Vajrayana vow.

The Tibetans' elaboration of the refuge formula reflects the fact that, unlike the fortunate early Buddhists who actually met Shakyamuni and were able to practice with the sole guidance of the Three Jewels, contemporary people encounter great obstacles to their practice and need every available source of refuge. (Lama)

17. See *'Phags-lam*, 108/6–109/1. The Bodhisattva vow is a verbal commitment to achieve enlightenment for the sake of all living beings, by practicing the Six Perfections (see pp. 106–109 and n. 45, below) and other aspects of the Bodhisattva training. See pp. 60–68.

18. See *'Phags-lam*, 109/1–3. The practitioner rejoices that by taking the Bodhisattva vow he has begun his career as a Bodhisattva.

19. See *'Phags-lam*, 109/3–4.

20. See *'Phags-lam*, 109/4–6.

21. Abridged in *'Phags-lam*, 109/6–7. See pp. 64–66.

22. More precisely, the body, speech and mind of all the enlightened beings dissolve into light and merge into Vajradhara. Vajradhara then dissolves into light and merges into your own body, speech and mind. (Lama)

23. "By virtue of my practice,
    May I soon attain Mahamudra,
    And place each sentient being, excluding none,
    In this same state."

This is one of many prayers for dedicating merit which may be used following any practice, by inserting the name of the goal of the practice in place of "Mahamudra."

Dedicating or sharing merit is the last act in all Mahayana practices. It increases the efficacy of any practice by transforming it from a samsaric act into one which leads to liberation. (Lama)

All religious practice accumulates merit for the practitioner. But if he tries to keep this merit for himself, he can unwittingly destroy it simply by

getting angry or using harsh words. But merit which has been dedicated
to all beings cannot be destroyed by any act of his. (Lama)

24. Blessing (*byin-rlabs*): process by which one individual introduces
some of his accumulated merit into another's "stream of being." The ability
to bestow blessing depends both on the donor's degree of spiritual attainment and on the recipient's faith. The donor is usually the root-guru, whose
blessing is said to contain that of all the sources of refuge combined.

Although future experiences are largely shaped by present actions, the
root-guru's blessing can partially modify this. That is, it can create conditions favorable to the maturation of any religious predispositions our past
actions may have generated, giving us the inspiration and energy we require
to begin practicing. In this way, unless our acts have been extremely unwholesome, the guru's blessing can help us overcome conflicting emotions
and other obstacles. (Lama)

The Lama used the simile, "Like the sun, enlightenment is always
present. Just as the sun's rays focused through a magnifying glass can burn
a piece of paper, enlightenment, 'focused' through the guru's blessing, can
destroy conflicting emotions. Thus, the guru's blessing helps us realize the
Buddha-potential we all possess." (Lama)

25. siddhi: attainment or power. The ordinary type includes worldly
influence or wealth. The supreme or special type is spiritual attainment,
such as Mahamudra realization.

Any yidam can bestow both types of siddhi to anyone who receives the
empowerment, meditates and recites the mantras and prayers for that yidam.
(Lama)

26. Buddha-activity: application of siddhi. For ordinary people, it is
physical, verbal or mental religious activity, including spreading the Dharma
and carrying out the Buddha's precepts. (Lama) For Buddhas, "It is scrip-
turally defined as the unbroken stream of spontaneous fulfillment of the
Bodhi-vows." (LPL)

The four types of Buddha-activity, which Deshung Rinpoche defines
as, "four types of mastery over one's samsaric situation, equivalent to ordinary siddhi, which may arise as a by-product of supreme siddhi," are: 1.
pacification of troublesome circumstances; 2. increase of wealth, intelligence,
store of merit, lifespan and other valuable samsaric commodities; 3. authority and influence over all types of beings, and 4. forceful dispersal of
disturbances caused by any samsaric phenomenon.

"Yogins of former times developed these techniques to an amazing
degree—they could fly through the air and so on—this is less common today. But these feats are nothing, compared to the development of bodhicitta,
the true goal of our practice." (Deshung Rinpoche, Interview, Feb. 20,
1975)

27. sku-gsum. The three kayas are not physical bodies, but symbols
of three ways in which Buddha acts, three "existential norms" which we
hope to achieve through religious practice.

The Nirmanakaya (*sprul-sku*, pronounced *tulku*) represents the variety of roles Buddha may play among ordinary people. He may appear for

example, as a type of art or artistic talent (*bzo-pa'i sprul-sku*); as an apparently ordinary being such as the Karmapa; or as a Buddha born in a given era, such as Shakyamuni. The latter is the "supreme" type of Nirmanakaya (*mchog-gi sprul-sku*). (Lama) The Nirmanakaya is often called the "transformation" or "illusory body" (*sgyu-lus*) because of its ability to appear and function exactly as do the beings around it. This enables Buddha to communicate with all types of beings and influence them most effectively.

The Sambhogakaya (*longs-spyod rdzogs-pa'i sku*) symbolizes Buddha's activity among higher Bodhisattvas. It's "five certainties" are: 1. The Sambhogakaya Buddha abides only in the highest Buddha-realm, where he 2. appears only as the Sambhogakaya, and 3. teaches only the Mahayana, while 4. surrounded only by tenth-level Bodhisattvas. 5. He abides until samsara is empty. (Lama)

The Sambhogakaya is sometimes characterized as "enlivening" (*srog-tsol*), because it excites and inspires beings to achieve Buddhahood. This life-enriching function is symbolized in iconography by depicting Sambhogakayas as splendidly attired royalty.

The Dharmakaya (*chos-sku*), the only one of the three considered to be ultimately real and thus incomprehensible through concepts, is pure transcending awareness (*ye-shes*), devoid of characteristics.

28. *lung-gi chos*: includes all scriptures to be read, learned and applied. (Lama)

29. *rtogs-pa'i chos*: the realization which comes with Buddhahood.

30. This is the community of fully enlightened beings. (Lama)

31. This is the community of those who have taken refuge or ordination, and Shravakas, Pratyekabuddhas and Arhats who have not yet reached full enlightenment. (Lama)

32. The Hinayana manner: 1. Taking Refuge in those not fully enlightened, such as Arhats, Shravakas or Pratyekabuddhas; 2. Taking Refuge for personal safety or liberation.

The worldly manner: Taking Refuge in samsaric beings, such as gods or demons. (Lama)

33. Symbols (*rten*, literally, "container"). *sku-rten*: statue or picture which in a sense "contains" the body of Buddha; *gsung-rten*: book or saying which "contains" his speech; *thugs-rten* or *mchod-rten* (Skt. *stupa*): container for relics of a Buddha or other enlightened being which represent Buddha's mind. (Lama)

34. *tsa-tsa*: miniature stupas or figures of Buddhas or other enlightened ones, made either from clay or ground bones from an animal you have eaten, pressed into a mould. If made of the latter, it brings blessing to the animal. (Lama)

35. These three prohibitions comprise the essential clause or "root" of the refuge vow. If they are violated, the vow is broken. According to Kalu Rinpoche, "heretics" here refers to irreligious people, i.e., those who doubt the possibility of liberation, the existence of enlightened ones and so on.

36. *Dam-pa'i chos padma dkar-po. bKa'-gyur*, P. 781.

37. Lay disciples (*dge-bsnyen;* Skt. *upasaka*) are those who have taken refuge and vowed to observe some or all of the five precepts which prohibit killing, stealing, lying, sexual misconduct and taking intoxicants.
"Counterfeit monks" are those who do not live up to their monastic vows. (LPL)
38. I.e., the enlightened attitude (bodhicitta).
39. "Eighty-four thousand" is the traditional number used to designate Buddha's teachings in their entirety.
40. *bKa'-gdams gzhung-drug*: six books used by that sect to prepare monks for, and train them in meditation. They include: 1. *Buddha-Jataka* (*sKyes-rabs. bKa'.,* P. 748); 2. an expanded version of the *Dhammapada,* called *Udanavarga* (*Tshoms. bKa'.,* P. 992; *bsTan-'gyur,* P. 5600); 3. Shantideva's *Bodhicaryavatara* (*Byang-chub spyod-'jug. bsTan.,* P. 5272); 4. *Siksasamuccaya* (*bsLab-pa kun-las btus-pa. bsTan.,* P. 5336); 5. *Bodhisattvabhumi* and *Sravakabhumi* (*Byang-chub sems-dpa'i sa* and *Nyan-thos-pa'i sa. bsTan.,* P. 5538 and 5537); and 6. *Mahayanasutralamkara* (*Theg-chen mdo-sde-rgyan. bsTan.,* P. 5521). (LPL)
41. Phadampa was an eleventh-century Kadampa teacher.
42. A superior person need never formally receive the Bodhisattva vow from a guru. He may simply recite it three times before symbols of the Three Jewels, or while visualizing them in the sky. However, aspirants are generally advised to take this beneficial vow as many times, and from as many gurus as possible. (Lama)
43. Since [Sahaja] Mahamudra is the highest practice in this system, it is used here to illustrate "perseverance," or application of the enlightened attitude, bodhicitta.
44. Even when engendering bodhicitta apart from the refuge practice, the sources of refuge are visualized to witness the Bodhisattva vow.
45. Six Perfections (*pha-rol tu phyin-pa;* Skt. *paramita*): Six "transcending functions" or clusters of attitudes and actions which help lead us (*phyin-pa*) to the "other shore" (*pha-rol tu*), i.e., Buddhahood. See H. V. Guenther's *Jewel Ornament,* pp. 148–231, and chapter 4, below.
46. Vows are commonly broken by overt actions. However, the Bodhisattva vow is exceptionally fragile, since it may be broken by mere thought. To preserve the vow, constant awareness of one's thoughts is essential. (Lama)
47. *shags,* pronounced "shah." There are two types: 1. *spyi-shags* or general Confession, and 2. *nyes-ltung-shags,* Confession of a specific misdeed, such as breaking the Bodhisattva vow.
One need not confess to one's guru or to any other person. Confession entails facing symbols of the sources of refuge or visualizing them, and 1. acknowledging the misdeed; 2. sincerely regretting it; and 3. resolving never to repeat it. Certain long prayers may be recited after Confession of violation of the Bodhisattva vow, but the prayer for the universal engenderment of bodhicitta (*'Phags-lam,* 109/3–4) will suffice.
After Confession, visualize the sources of refuge dissolving into light, and then into yourself. Then, let your mind rest without conceptualizing, for as long as possible. (Lama)

48. Killing, stealing, lying about spiritual attainments and indulging in sex. (LPL)

49. A yana is a particular style of religious career or path. Here, the Shravakayana, Pratyekabuddhayana and Mahayana are meant.

50. *bLo-gros rgya-mtsho zhus-pa'i mdo. bKa'.,* P. 819.

51. Bodhisattvas.

52. *bdag-gzhan mnyam-brje.* For detailed instructions on this practice, see Kongtrul's *Theg-pa chen-po blo-sbyong don bdun-ma, gDams-ngag-mdzod,* vol. 3. Delhi: N. Lungtok and N. Gyaltsan, 1971, fols. 181–213, translated by Ken McLeod as *A Direct Path to Enlightenment.* Vancouver: Kagyu Kunkhyab Chuling, 1975. Also see below, "Sending and Receiving."

53. *mi-ma-yin:* troublesome spirits who may appear human.

54. Since he has not meditated with a correct attitude, this person will neither develop bodhicitta nor come to act as a Bodhisattva. (LPL) The "insubstantial meditative experience" (*nyams-myong mag-mog*) is that of a person who cultivates only the first type of moral conduct, i.e., wholesome action (particularly meditation) pertaining to himself alone.

Fig. 1. Vajrasattva.

3 SECOND OF THE FOUR SPECIAL FOUNDATIONS

The Hundred-Syllable Mantra of Vajrasattva Which Purifies Harmful Deeds and Removes Obscurations

[After Taking Refuge and Engendering the Enlightened Attitude, the newly committed aspirant is symbolically purified by practicing the meditation and reciting the mantra of the Buddha Vajrasattva (Dorje Sempa). This purification insures the efficacy of his future religious endeavors.

The impurities to be removed include the accumulated influences of all the unwholesome thoughts, words and deeds he has perpetrated throughout his samsaric career, as well as their cause: ignorance or bewilderment.

While this purification removes past unwholesomeness, it does not insure the individual against future defilement. Any new unwholesome act necessitates Confession (see pp. 84–85 and chap. 2, n. 47) and renewed purification prior to further religious practice. Therefore, recitation of Vajrasattva's mantra normally precedes other Vajrayana rituals.

According to Kalu Rinpoche, the efficacy of this practice is greatly enhanced if one has first received its empowerment. In the empowerment ritual, the guru plays the part of Vajrasattva. Using ritual implements, scented water and incense, he purifies the aspirant for the first time.

The Vajrasattva practice involves the following steps:

1. Sitting cross-legged before an icon of Vajrasattva, chanting his liturgical description and visualizing him seated on your head.

2. Praying to him for purification.

3. Chanting the description and visualizing the process of purification.

4. Reciting the hundred-syllable mantra while counting the number of recitations on a rosary.

5. Reciting prayers of confession.

6. Imagining Vajrasattva's conferral of blessing.

7. Dissolving the visualization and letting the mind rest.

8. Dedicating merit.]

PROLOGUE

Generally speaking, two "hundred-syllable" mantras exist. One is the "hundred-syllable mantra of the Tathagata," which is said to come from the *Trisamayavyuharaja tantra*.[1] The other is the "hundred-syllable mantra of Vajrasattva (Dorje Sempa)," which is taught in many tantras.

[The hundred-syllable mantra] of Vajrasattva exists in two forms. The first is the "hundred-syllable name-mantra"[2] which incorporates the boundless family of peaceful deities who are beyond samsara. The second is the "hundred-syllable mantra of the wrathful *heruka*," said to come from the *Abhidhanottara tantra*.[3] These mantras are known as "hundred-syllable" mantras by our school of the Mantrayana despite the fact that they may actually contain either more or less than one hundred syllables.

At this time we will describe, in stages, the visualization which accompanies the peaceful Vajrasattva's hundred-syllable mantra.

There are two different ways of visualizing [the peaceful Vajrasattva]: 1. Alone, as a universal ruler,[4] according to the *yoga-tantra;* 2. in sexual embrace, according to the *anuttarayoga-tantra*.[5] Here we will follow the *yoga-tantra*.

PRACTICAL INSTRUCTIONS

VISUALIZATION AND MANTRA

[As you recite the descriptive liturgy,][6] think: On the crown of your head is the syllable 𑀧 (*Paṁ*), which changes into a lotus. Above the lotus is an ཨ (*A*) which changes into a moon [lying flat]. Resting on top of the lotus and moon is a 𑁆 (*Hūṁ*), which changes into a white, five-pronged vajra marked with a 𑁆 where the prongs converge. Light radiates out from this 𑁆 as an offering to the Noble Ones, benefiting sentient beings and then returning [into the 𑁆 . The entire vajra] changes into Vajrasattva, who is not separate from your own root-guru.

His body is white with one face and two hands. His right hand holds a five-pronged [golden] vajra at his heart. His left holds a silver bell at his side.

He sits in the Bodhisattva posture[7] with his right foot slightly extended and his left folded inward. His upper and lower garments are of precious silks. He wears the jewelled diadem and the other peaceful ornaments. On the crown of his head, on his topknot sits his guru, [the Buddha] Akshobhya (Michodpa), symbol of his family.[8]

His body, adorned with the [thirty-two] major and [eighty] minor marks [of physical perfection], is clear and emits measureless light. It appears to lack all substantiality, like a reflection of the moon in water. Three syllables are located at the three places.[9]

Above the lotus and moon, encircling a white 𑖮 at his heart like a snake coiled clockwise, is the string of white letters of his hundred-syllable mantra, facing outward and beginning in front of [the 𑖮].

Light radiates from the mantra, inviting the Buddhas of the ten directions and three times and their sons. They all dissolve [into Vajrasattva], who thus becomes the unity of all the Precious Ones.[10]

Pray to him[11] for the removal of harmful acts and obscurations.[12]

[Chant the liturgy[13] and visualize the process of purification]: The [white] elixir pours down from the seed-syllable [𑖮] and circle of mantra-letters at his heart, filling up his entire form. The excess streams out through the big toe of his right foot and enters [your body] in the form of light, through the crown of your head.

All the harmful deeds and obscurations you have gathered throughout your beginningless lifetimes, such as violations of sacred commitments and so on, take the form of soot and sludge. All diseases [infecting your body] take the form of pus and blood. All the demons [inhabiting your body] take the forms of different insects.

All the substances [comprising your physical body], including flesh and blood, are carried along like chunks of ice in frothy waters and eliminated through the orifices of the sense-organs and the pores, to dissolve into the mighty golden ground.[14]

Visualize that after your body has been purified by the elixir of awareness, the excess elixir overflows [at the crown of your head] and comes in contact with Vajrasattva's foot.

Visualize this very clearly again and again. It is said: "If your mind is distracted [during visualization], recitation [of the mantra] even for a kalpa will be fruitless." Thus, do the visualization without a moment's distraction while continuously reciting the hundred or the six-syllable mantra[15] clearly and softly, at a moderate pace.

Finally, join your palms [in front of you] in a gesture of devotion.

Recite the Prayers of Confession beginning, "Lord, because of my ignorance . . ."[16]

Then, pleased by your recitation, the smiling Vajrasattva calls out, "Oh son of good family, all your harmful deeds, obscurations and transgressions are purified from this day forth."

Then he dissolves into light which melts into yourself. Now, Vajrasattva's body, speech and mind are non-separate from your own body, speech and mind. Let your mind rest without conceptualizing.

At the close of each meditation session, dedicate the merit.

SIGNS OF SUCCESSFUL PRACTICE

The signs of the purification of your harmful acts are elucidated in the authoritative treatises [of this tradition]. In particular, it is said that you will experience a feeling of physical buoyancy, little need for sleep, good health, clear thinking and glimpses of realization.

COMMENTARY

The general message of this practice is: Abandon all harmful deeds; perform wholesome ones.

Only the perfect Buddha knew what to reject and what to adopt and demonstrated this to others. One who has deep faith in his teachings and applies them has grasped their inmost significance.

ACTION AND RESULT

Although a wholesome or harmful act may have been minute while it was still a mere motivation, by the time it yields its result it will have grown considerably. Harmful deeds lead to miserable states of existence; wholesome deeds lead to happy ones. None of your deeds will be impotent. You will not experience the results of that which you have not done.

THE SOURCE OF ALL ACTIONS

Actions which are wholly motivated by attachment, aversion and stupidity but have not assumed a concrete physical or verbal form are mental actions. Those which have assumed concrete form are physical or verbal actions. All actions begin as mental actions. Therefore it is said: "The mind is the source of the poison which leads the world into darkness."

"Harmful action" includes the "five most heinous acts," "five less heinous acts," "ten unwholesome acts," "four burdens," "eight perversions" and others.[17] "Harmful action" also includes breaking any of the three types of vows [Hinayana, Mahayana, or Vajrayana], encouraging others to do so and delighting in or praising the violation.

In short, not only do you carry around the heap of wrongdoing accrued in beginningless past lives, but you add to it in this life. Most of your motives, influenced by the three poisons, become concrete physical, verbal and mental acts.

Even in this life, gods and men will curse and slander you for your bad deeds. You will be besieged by sorrows. Your protecting deities will grow lazy, and demons will take advantage of this and obstruct [your religious practice]. You will join the lower classes of men. Living in the shadow of your bad deeds, you will have bad luck. Even your dreams will be bad. You will be unhappy. Potentially fatal accidents will occur, and severe illness will attack you.

You will experience the miseries of a fearful death, and of terrible visions in the bardo.

After death [and rebirth] you will undergo a long period of suffering in the three lower realms, in proportion to your great, moderate or small misdeeds.

Even if you are reborn in the higher realms, your life will be brief and disease-ridden.

You will be hated by hostile enemies, although you have done them no harm. Your homeland will be plagued by epidemics, crop failure and war.

Because of the similarity between cause and result, you will be naturally inclined to do harm, and your suffering will continually and uninterruptedly increase.

You are absolutely wrong [if you imagine] any harmful act to be necessary or profitable. [You are mistaken if you think that you *must* commit one] to subdue enemies or protect friends, or for money, property, fame, food, clothes etc. No matter how rich you are in these things, at death they will be of less use than a sesame seed! You will not be able to take along a morsel of food or scrap of clothing, to say nothing of your fame, wealth, son, wife and the rest.

When you wander alone in the lower realms, the painful consequences of your harmful acts cannot be transferred to others: you alone must suffer them!

[Think as follows: "In this uncertain world], enemies may become friends and friends may easily become enemies. I, who have dared to do harm, have been seized by Maras, possessed by harmful spirits and become a dull-witted and ignorant person. In the past, I never thought about the consequences [of my acts], nor did it ever occur to me to refuse [to act harmfully]. Since death may come at any time, I may not even have time to purify my harmful acts! If I have no time to purify

them, what awful miseries await me in the lower realms when death
takes me away!" There is no harm in being driven by self-disgust. Meditate unhappily. *renunciation*

Furthermore, concealed misdeeds grow larger and larger, as the
seeds of harmful acts are mixed with the water and manure of deception.

If you do not conceal your faults but recognize them and reveal
your sad state to others, your faults will not grow but will weaken, for
"The truth curtails."

Harmful acts may be easily uprooted by strenuous application of
the means of purification of misdeeds: intense regret and sincere Confession. When you perfect the use of these skillful means, even one
wholesome deed will have the capacity to undo heaps of harmful ones.

CONFESSION   *Admission vs Confession*

To say "I committed this misdeed" is to admit wrongdoing. To say so
with strong regret and mental anguish is to confess. To confess is to regard with reverence and wonder those who have not committed such
misdeeds, to feel remorse and shame for your own misdeeds and to directly and sincerely pray: "Regard me with compassion, and purify this
deed of mine."

THE FOUR POWERS

[Your Confession will be effective if you apply the four powers]:

1. The "power to renounce" and regret your previous misdeeds as
vigorously as if you had swallowed poison.

2. The "power to refuse to repeat a harmful deed," and to firmly
resolve, "Even if my life is at stake, I will never do it again."

3. The "power to rely" on Taking Refuge and Engendering the
Enlightened Attitude.

4. The "power to carry out all types of remedial wholesome acts to
purify harmful ones," including the "Six Gates of Remedy [see below],"
and others.

You should apply all four powers.

[Be aware of the following]:

1. If you merely go through the motions of Confession, without
regretting your past misdeeds, these deeds will not be purified.

2. If you have not vowed against future misdeeds, all your Confession and wholesome action will be pointless.

3. A single Confession by one who has truly taken refuge and en-

gendered the enlightened attitude has more power to purify harmful acts than a hundred thousand Confessions by one who has not taken refuge or engendered the enlightened attitude. Furthermore, one day of Confession by one who has received [Vajrayana] empowerment[18] clears away more harmful acts than many years of Confession by one who has taken only [Hinayana or Mahayana vows]. This is because [Vajrayana empowerment] greatly increases the power of reliance.

4. The same applies to increasing your wholesome acts and [eliminating] harmful ones.

THE SIX GATES OF REMEDY

1. To remove karmic obscurations, say the name of Amitabha (Opamay), Bhaishajyaguru (Menla), Akshobhya (Mitrugpa) and other Buddhas and Bodhisattvas known for their ability to remove karmic obscurations, and recite their names to others.

2. Set up images, holy books and stupas, [symbols of Buddha's body, speech and mind].

3. Make offerings to the above three symbols; serve the Sangha; offer the mandala [of the universe].[19] If you have joined the Mantrayana, practice chilkor[20] meditations and participate in community offering festivals.[21] Especially, honor the guru with the "five pleasing offerings."[22]

4. Recite the sutras and tantras taught by the Buddha, such as the Prajnaparamita and Mahaparinirvana sutras.

5. Recite the "hundred-syllable mantra of the Tathagata," the mantras of Vairocana (Kunrig), Akshobhya, and other profound mantras.

6. Confident in the potentiality for Buddhahood, meditate on the significance of non-self. Recite [Vajrasattva's mantra] without regard for the "three spheres":[23] 1. obscurations to be purified, 2. an instrument of purification (the deity's mantra) and 3. a purifier (yourself). This is the application of profound openness. After meditation sessions, concentrate on the unreality, the illusoriness [of all phenomena].

THE HUNDRED-SYLLABLE MANTRA OF VAJRASATTVA

Any of these six remedies, if sincerely applied, can [eventually] destroy the causes and results of harmful action. For immediate purification of the formidable misdeeds and obscurations which block Mahamudra realization—the very ground—we have explained the meditation and mantra of Vajrasattva.

Since they have been so recently accumulated, the obscurations and

misdeeds we have gathered in this life greatly obstruct meditative experience. Violations of the three vows [Hinayana, Mahayana and Vajra-
yana] are particularly [obstructive]; transgressions against your guru's
body, speech and mind are even more so. [Misdeeds such as] violation
of other sacred Mantrayana commitments, trading images for cash or
food, etc., tend to cloud earlier meditative experiences and inhibit new
ones.

The hundred-syllable mantra of Vajrasattva is the most praiseworthy
[of all remedies] because it clears away all such misdeeds. According to
Lord Atisha:

> Just as a freshly cleaned mandala placed in a very dusty spot immedi-
> ately becomes covered with dust again, many minor violations of Mantra-
> yana [commitments] constantly crop up.[24]

If you ask [in despair], "Will the time never come when the path
[to enlightenment] will truly become part of me?", the answer is: The
Mantrayana employs a great variety of skillful means. Although you have
committed many minor transgressions of the Mantrayana, employing just
one of these means for one moment will purify them all! For this reason,
we have provided a detailed account of the meditation and hundred-
syllable mantra of Vajrasattva.

IN PRAISE OF THE HUNDRED-SYLLABLE MANTRA

The measureless immediate and ultimate benefits [of reciting Vajrasattva's mantra] are unanimously proclaimed in both the new and old
tantras. An Indian work sums it all up:

> Though they embody the five transcending awarenesses,
> Practices called dharani, mantra, mudra, stupa and mandala,
> Do not amass the merit of one recitation of the hundred-syllable
>   mantra.
> Whoever chants the hundred syllables
> Is said to gather merit equal to
> That which adorns all Buddhas,
> Numerous as motes of dust.

And further:

> Whoever chants the hundred syllables
> Is struck by neither sickness, pain, nor early death.

Whoever chants the hundred syllables
Is not beset by poverty or woe.
His enemies are crushed and
All his wishes are fulfilled.

Whoever chants the hundred syllables
Obtains a son if a son he wants,
Or wealth if wealth he wants.
If land he lacks, then land he gains.

Whoever wants longevity
Should chant the hundred syllables,
And, when he thinks his years are spent,
He'll find three hundred more are sent!
The same man, happy in this world,
In Sukhavati[25] will be born.

Whoever chants the hundred syllables,
Is safe from *khandro, jungpo, rolang,*
And from demons of forgetfulness.[26]

If they recite the hundred syllables,
Evildoers, too, will see the Buddha.

If he recites the hundred syllables,
A fool will gain intelligence,
A luckless man turn fortunate.
Change and frustration will be destroyed,
The worst wrongdoer, purified.

In this and other lives as well,
He will a *cakravartin*[27] be,
And finally, in freedom rest,
And Buddhahood attain.

It is said that if you strenuously [practice this meditation and recite this mantra] your minor and moderate misdeeds will be completely puri-fied. Your major misdeeds will not increase but be suppressed and gradually purified.

Generally speaking, if you truly believe in [the doctrine of] action and result you will inevitably regret your harmful deeds. Then your Confession will be genuine.

All this seems to imply that realization will inevitably follow purifi-cation. But those of us who merely mouth the prayers and affect the practices of the monastic life, without true faith or regret, will achieve no more realization than a tortoise has hair.[28]

NOTES

1. *Dam-tshig-gsum bkod-kyi rgyud. bKa'.*, P. 134. A *kriya-tantra*. The mantra invokes the name of Shakyamuni. (LPL)

2. "Name-mantras" or "adaptable name-mantras," including all the mantras mentioned here, consist of a basic mantra into which the name of any Buddha, yidam or other enlightened being may be inserted. There is one basic version of the mantra for peaceful, and another for wrathful deities. In the present mantra, Vajrasattva stands for all peaceful yidams combined. (LPL)

3. *mNgon-brjod bla-ma'i rgyud. bKa'.*, P. 17. "Heruka" is a generic term for wrathful male yidams. Here it denotes the wrathful aspect of Vajrasattva. (LPL)

4. See chapter 4, n. 19.

5. See H. V. Guenther's *Naropa*, pp. 131–34.

6. See *'Phags-lam*, 109/7–110/1.

7. A more relaxed posture than Vajradhara's vajra posture of deep meditation.

8. Vajrasattva is Akshobhya's Sambhogakaya form.

9. 1. a white ཨོཾ (Oṁ) at the eyes; 2. a red ཨཱཿ (Āḥ) at the throat; 3. a blue ཧཱུཾ (Hūṁ) at the heart.

10. Here, *'Phags-lam* instructs: "Meditate that light from his heart invites the *ye-shes-pas*. They dissolve [into him] and he becomes the essence of all the Precious Ones combined." (110/1)

The incorporation of all enlightened beings into the visualized deity makes him a truly effective purifier. (Lama)

11. See *'Phags-lam*, 110/1–2.

12. For "harmful acts" see n. 17, below.

Obscurations (*sgrib-pa*; Skt. *avarana*) are of two general types: 1. *klesha-avarana*: emotional obscurations, which drive us to precipitous action; 2. *jneya-avarana*: intellectual obscurations or ignorance, which prevent us from seeing things as they are.

For a more detailed classification of obscurations, see chapter 5, n. 24, and pp. 121–122.

13. See *'Phags-lam*, 110/2–3.

14. See chapter 4, n. 14.

At this point the meditator should imagine that he retains only the insubstantial, clear "rainbow-body" (*'ja'-lus*) of an enlightened being, which is like a transparent container, now filled with the white elixir. (Lama)

15. See *'Phags-lam*, 110/3–5.

Recitation of the long version is required when the mantras are being counted to complete 111,111 recitations. At other times the short version may be used. (LPL)

16. See *'Phags-lam,* 110/5–7.

17. The "five most heinous acts" (often called the "five inexpiables"), literally, "five acts which bring immediate retribution": matricide, parricide, killing an Arhat or guru, creating discord in the Sangha, and willfully wounding a Tathagata.

The "five less heinous acts": killing a novice or monk, seducing a monk or nun, destroying or mutilating images of Buddha, scriptures or shrine-rooms.

The ten unwholesome acts have been explained in chapter 1, section 3.

The "four burdens" (or "weighty acts") consist of four sets of acts: 1. Four burdens of perversity: a. Looking down on learned people; b. treating holy persons, monks or nuns in a condescending manner; c. stealing food belonging to someone in meditation retreat; d. stealing a yogin's ritual implements. 2. Four burdens of degeneracy: a. Swearing in order to conceal your guilt; b. violating the Shravaka precepts; c. the Bodhisattva precepts; d. tantric precepts. 3. Four burdens of verbal abuse: a. Denouncing sacred images; b. belittling the knowledge of learned people; c. deriding words of truth; d. engaging in religious polemics out of prejudice. 4. Four burdens of blasphemy: a. Holding perverted views; b. injuring a holy person; c. insulting your equals; d. accusing an innocent person of wrongdoing. (LPL)

The "eight perversions": despising the wholesome, glorifying the unwholesome, disturbing truth-seekers, abandoning your spiritual teacher, dividing the Sangha, abandoning spiritual brothers and sisters, and desecrating a sacred mandala. (LPL)

18. See chapter 5, n. 19.

19. See chapter 4.

20. Chilkor (*dkyil-'khor*) is the usual Tibetan translation of the Sanskrit "mandala." Kongtrul, however, uses "chilkor" and the Tibetan transliteration of the Sanskrit "mandala" to denote different things. "Mandala" refers to a symbol of the universe offered to the sources of refuge, as in chapter 4, below.

"Chilkor" refers to a symbolic "map" of enlightenment used in certain Vajrayana practices. In this type of symbol, the highest Buddha figure which represents the ultimate goal, is placed at the center. It is surrounded by concentric rings of yidams who represent that goal as it appears to the aspirant at various stages of his spiritual development.

21. Devotional services of prayer, chanting, offering and feasting by tantric gurus and their close disciples.

22. 1. Show him respect; 2. offer him service and needed goods; 3. have faith and confidence in him; 4. obey him; 5. practice Dharma. (LPL)

23. *'khor-gsum dmigs-med.* Any action is said to involve three components or "spheres": 1. an object; 2. an instrument; 3. a subject or actor. Religious acts performed in a spirit of disinterestedness, with no preconceptions about any of these spheres or about the outcome of the action, are unaffected by conflicting emotions and therefore conducive to liberation.

24. Since the meditation and mantra of Vajrasattva renews broken vows, it is especially valuable to the Mantrayanist, whose vows are so fragile.

25. This man's wishes are fulfilled beyond his expectations.

Sukhavati (Dewachen) is Buddha Amitabha's blissful paradise. Buddha realms are not simply places of enjoyment, but are the best possible conditions for religious practice and instruction.

26. These *khandro* (*mkha'-'gro*) are not the enlightened *ye-shes mkha'-'gro* of the refuge tree, but samsaric demons called *sha-za mkha'-'gro* or flesh-eating dakinis.

Jungpo (*'byung-po*) is a general term for "demon."

Rolang (*ro-langs*, literally, "risen corpses") are corpses which have been reanimated either by ritual or invading spirits. See T. Wylie, "Ro-langs: the Tibetan Zombie," *History of Religions*, 4, no. 1: 69–80.

27. See chap. 4, n. 19.

28. I.e., none.

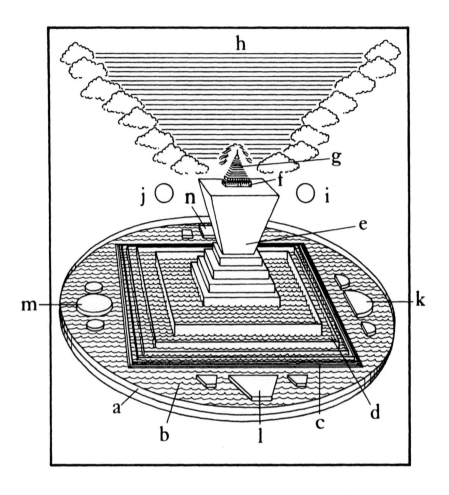

Fig. 2. Traditional depiction of the main features of the Ideal Universe.

a. iron mountain
b. ocean
c. seven rings of mountains
d. seven lakes
e. Mt. Meru
f. city of Vishnu
g. Indra's palace

h. deva-realms
i. sun
j. moon
k. Videha and satellites
l. Jambudvipa and satellites
m. Godaniya and satellites
n. Uttara-Kuru and satellites

4 THIRD OF THE FOUR SPECIAL FOUNDATIONS

The Mandala-Offering Which Perfects the Two Accumulations

[In preparation for the Guru-Yoga and further practices, the aspirant must be purged of negative qualities and enriched with positive ones. The purging is achieved by the Vajrasattva ritual of the previous chapter; the enrichment, by the Mandala-Offering which "perfects" the Two Accumulations. These are the Accumulation of Merit and the Accumulation of Transcending Awareness.

"Merit" refers to the cumulative effects of meritorious actions (see chap. 1, Action, Cause, and Result).

Transcending Awareness is direct understanding of ultimate reality.

PERFECTION OF THE TWO ACCUMULATIONS

Accumulation of Merit	*Accumulation of Awareness*
1. Perfection of generosity	6. Perfection of Insight
2. Perfection of moral conduct	
3. Perfection of patience	
4. Perfection of strenuousness	
5. Perfection of meditative concentration.	
= *Skillful Means*	= *Insight*

As illustrated above, "perfection" or complete acquisition of the Two Accumulations is equivalent both to the fulfillment of the Six Perfections and the integration of skillful means (compassion) and insight (realization of emptiness), the goals of the Mahayana and Vajrayana respectively.

In this practice, the aspirant perfects his Accumulation of Merit by the supremely meritorious act of repeatedly offering the entire universe to the sources of refuge. He perfects his Accumulation of Transcending Awareness by maintaining the understanding that this offering, its recipients and the giver himself are not things-in-themselves but empty.

A short version of this practice is generally performed at the start of
Vajrayana rituals. In it, the "mandala mudra" is used to symbolize the universe (see Beyer, *Cult of Tara,* p. 168).

Throughout this chapter, the word mandala has four referents: 1. the
metal disk (resembling an inverted pie plate) on which the piles of rice
are placed; 2. the piles of rice (*tsombu*); 3. the visualization and 4. the
three together.

Practice of the Mandala-Offering entails:

A. Preparation of the *drubpay* (*sgrub-pa'i*) *mandala,* the preliminary
mandala representing the sources of refuge. This involves:

1. Holding a metal disk in the left hand while cleaning it by three
clockwise strokes with the inner part of the right wrist, and reciting two
purificatory mantras.

2. Placing five piles of rice on the disk and visualizing them as the
five sources of refuge, while reciting the descriptive liturgy.

3. Imagining the union of these deities with the "real" sources of
refuge.

4. Placing the drubpay mandala on a high covered table or altar.

B. Preparation of the *chodpay* (*mchod-pa'i*) *mandala,* representing the
ideal universe, and offering it to the sources of refuge. This involves:

1. Holding a second disk in the left hand while cleaning it as before and purifying it by reciting Vajrasattva's mantra.

2. Chanting the "ground" mantra, sprinkling perfumed water on
the disk and visualizing it as the golden ground.

3. Chanting the "rim" mantra, dropping rice around the rim of
the disk and visualizing it as the circular iron mountain which surrounds
the universe.

4. Chanting the descriptive liturgy while dropping piles of rice on
the disk and visualizing them as the thirty-seven features of the ideal
universe.

5. Reciting a four-line offering prayer, praying for acceptance of
the Mandala-Offering and for universal enlightenment.

6. Reciting the mandala mantra, tossing some rice into the air and
praying for achievement of the aims of the Mandala-Offering.

7. Clearing the rice off the disk.

8. Reciting the four-line offering prayer and dropping piles of rice
on the disk to represent the simplified universe of seven features, while
visualizing the same elaborate universe as before.

9. Clearing the rice off the disk and repeating steps 8 and 9 as
many times as desired for the session.

10. Praying for the attainment of Mahamudra and reciting the
Seven Branches of Religious Service and the concluding prayer.

11. Dedicating merit.

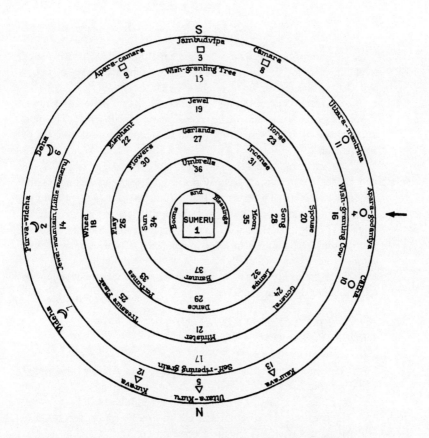

Fig. 3. F. D. Lessing's Diagram of the Mandala of the Universe of thirty-seven features, for construction (from *Yung-ho-kung,* p. 106). The numbers indicate the order in which the piles of rice are to be dropped on the mandala-disk. The practitioner imagines he is facing east (arrow).

The practice is complete when 111,111 long or short chodpay mandalas have been offered.]

PRACTICAL INSTRUCTIONS

CONSTRUCTION OF MANDALAS

There is nothing wrong with offering a small mandala if it is made of some fine material, such as precious metal. But a mandala made of a poor material, such as clay or wood, ought to be large.[1]

If you lack [such materials], you may use a slab of wood or stone. If you lack even these, a mentally-created mandala will suffice. The most important thing is the visualization [which accompanies construction of any mandala].

You will need two mandala disks. Use the finer or larger of the two [as the base for the] drubpay mandala. Use the other one for the chodpay mandala. [To construct both mandalas] use piles of gold or silver (best), conch or cowrie shell (second best), or rice grains (acceptable), each moistened with scented water. If you can afford it, use fresh grains each time [you offer a mandala]. If you cannot, replace some of the grains with fresh ones put aside for this purpose.

These grains are not for your own later consumption but should be offered to the Precious Ones.[2]

CONSTRUCTION AND VISUALIZATION OF THE DRUBPAY MANDALA

Focus your attention on the drubpay mandala and clean it three times[3] while reciting the mantras: "Oṁ Vajra Amrita Hūṁ Phat," and "Oṁ Svabhāva Shuddha Sarva Dharma Svabhāva Shuddho Haṁ."[4]

Meditate that out of emptiness the mandala appears as a magnificent palace endowed with all the special attributes.[5]

[Recite the liturgy describing the sources of refuge].[6]

At the center of the disk, place five small piles of rice. Visualize these as the five sources of refuge, just as they were in the Refuge meditation except that the lake and the wish-fulfilling tree may be omitted, and the dharmapalas are placed among [the five sources, instead of below them].

Light radiates from the three seed-syllables located at the three places,[7] inviting the numberless "awareness deities" [to come forth from the Dharmadhatu], their natural abode. Meditate that each ["awareness deity" and each visualized deity] merge into one.[8] Place the mandala on a high, covered table in front of you, and pray that the deities be present. Surround it with the five types of offerings,[9] if you possess them.

If you do not have a drubpay mandala disk, or if you perform the Mandala-Offering very regularly, simply meditate that the deities to whom you are about to offer it are present in the sky before you [as in the Refuge visualization].

CONSTRUCTION AND VISUALIZATION OF THE CHODPAY MANDALA

Then, hold the chodpay mandala disk in your left hand and flower petals [or some scented water] in your right. Recite the hundred-syllable mantra [of Vajrasattva] while you dust the mandala three times in a clockwise direction [just as you cleaned the drubpay mandala]. Meditate that the illnesses, misfortunes, bad deeds, obscurations and impurities of yourself and others, of the world and its inhabitants, which have all arisen due to clinging to external objects and an internal mind—all these are wholly and completely removed. Just like the mind, whose nature is stainless, your mandala must be clean, utterly free of dirt and impurities.

Since this Mandala-Offering is of great consequence, you must use the finest materials you can afford and carry out the practice with the utmost cleanliness.[10]

Two different arrangements of the universe are commonly used for the main visualization. One is based on the *Kalacakra tantra*[11] and the other on the Abhidharma literature. Because Mahamudra is the consummation of the essentials of all the tantras, in practicing these Foundations [of Mahamudra] it makes no difference which of the two you use.[12] However, our visualization follows the Abhidharma version, since it is so well known.

VISUALIZATION AND CONSTRUCTION OF THE MANDALA OF THE UNIVERSE OF THIRTY-SEVEN FEATURES

While reciting the mantra "Oṁ Vajra Bhūmi Āḥ Hūṁ," sprinkle the mandala disk with the scented water [which you have been holding in your right hand], to represent its being moistened with the "dew" of bodhicitta. If you do not have scented water, scatter flower petals [on the disk].

Meditate that the mandala disk is the wide and spacious golden ground, with plains smooth as the palm of your hand and an ocean whose swirling, fragrant waters have the eight fine attributes.[13] You need not visualize the circles of water and wind beneath the ground.[14]

While reciting the mantra "Oṁ Vajra Rekhe Āḥ Hūṁ," scatter rice counterclockwise around the rim [of the disk, with your right hand] to represent the iron mountain, and meditate that this *is* the circular iron mountain which surrounds [the universe].

In some versions of this practice you would now recite "Hum" and place a drop of scented water or a circle of petals at the center [of the mandala]. In the present version this will not be done.

Similarly, in some versions you would visualize Mt. Meru and the other [topographical features] growing out of various seed-syllables. But in this version you meditate that they are complete from the moment you call them to mind.

Gradually chant the words[15] as you meditate on their meaning.

In the midst of the ocean stands the four-sided Mt. Meru[1][16] with its base of four square steps and its square peak, which is widest at the top. Its eastern slope is made of crystal, its southern of lapis lazuli, its western of ruby, its northern of emerald. The lakes, sky and continents [surrounding Meru] reflect the colors of each of its slopes.[17]

At its borders are the seven four-sided, hollow, gold mountains which surround Mt. Meru. [Beginning with the mountain closest to Meru], each one is half as high as the preceding one. [The mountains are called] Yugandhara, Ishadhara, Khadiraka, Sudarshana, Ashvakama, Vinataka and Nimindhara.

Interspersed among these mountains are the [seven Sitas, square] swirling lakes whose waters have the eight fine attributes. They are full of wish-fulfilling gems and other treasures belonging to the *nagas* [who inhabit them].[18]

In the ocean surrounding all this, [are the four great continents and their satellite continents]. Videha [2], in the east, is white and semi-circular. Jambudvipa [3], in the south, is blue and trapezoidal. Godaniya [4], in the west, is red and round. Uttara-Kuru [5], in the north, is green and square.

Each of the four main continents has two similarly shaped and colored "satellite" continents, one to its left and one to its right. [Videha

a. the precious wheel   b. the precious wish-fulfilling gem

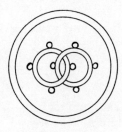
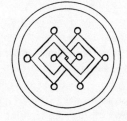

c. the earrings of   d. the earrings of   e. the tusks of the
    the precious queen   the precious minister   precious elephant

f. the horn of the   g. the badge of
precious Unicorn (or horse)   the precious general

Fig. 4. The Symbols of the Seven Possessions of the Cakravartin.

has Deha [6] and Videha [7]; Jambudvipa has Camara [8] and Upaca-mara [9]; Apara-Godaniya has Shatha [10] and Uttara-mantrina [11]; and Uttara-Kuru has Kurava [12] and Kaurava [13]].

In the four continents, above Mt. Meru, and in the various quarters of the sky are:

[In the eastern sky], the mountain of jewels [14], made of dia-mond, lapis lazuli, sapphire, emerald, pearl, gold, silver and [clear] crystal.

[In the southern sky], the grove of wish-fulfilling trees [15] from which everything desired falls like rain.

[In the western sky], the herd of wish-fulfilling cows [16] from whose every pore springs anything you desire.

[In the northern sky], the inexhaustible, satisfying food which grows without cultivation [17].

There are also the "seven possessions of the *cakravartin*":[19]

The thousand-spoked wheel [18] [in the eastern sky] is made of gold from the river Jambud.

The eight-sided wish-fulfilling gem [19] [in the southern sky] is bright as the sun's rays and can be seen to shine from a distance of sev-eral *yojanas*.

The beautiful queen [20] [in the western sky] possesses the thirty-two marks of feminine perfection.

The minister [21] [in the northern sky] excels in both physique and intelligence, and can find treasures buried underground.

The golden-necklaced white elephant [22] [in the southeastern sky] with his seven steadfast limbs[20] can carry [the *cakravartin*] anywhere at all.

The excellent horse [23] [in the southwestern sky], who is colored like a peacock's neck, can circle the four continents in an instant.

The mighty general [24] [in the northwestern sky] possesses the sixty-four special skills.

There is a beautiful treasure-vase [25] [in the northwestern sky] containing inexhaustible quantities of jewels of seven kinds, including sapphires and others.

[There are eight goddesses with offerings].

The white goddess of laughter [26] [in the eastern sky] stands in the *vajra-mushti-sandhi* posture.[21]

The yellow goddess of garlands [27] [in the southern sky] holds garlands of flowers and jewels.

a. precious parasol   b. golden fish   c. vase

d. lotus   e. white conch shell

f. magnificent knot   g. banner of victory   h. golden wheel

Fig. 5. The Eight Auspicious Symbols.

The red and white goddess of music [28] [in the western sky] plays a *vina*.[22]

The green goddess of dance [29] [in the northern sky] is dancing.

The yellow flower-goddess [30] [in the southeastern sky] holds a bouquet of flowers.

The white incense-goddess [31] [in the southwestern sky] holds a censer of burning incense.

The red goddess of lamps [32] [in the northwestern sky] holds a butter-lamp.

The green goddess of perfume [33] [in the northeastern sky] holds a conch shell of perfume.

In the northeastern sky above Mt. Meru is the fiery crystal disk of the sun [34] emitting brilliant rays. [In the southwestern sky above Meru] is the cool, refreshing disk of the moon [35].[23] The palaces of planets and stars emit their varied radiances.

In the center of the flat top of Mt. Meru is Indra's palace (Vaijayanta) in Vishnu's city, Sudarshana. At the four corners of this city are Caitraratha and the rest of the four parks. [In these parks] are Pariyatra and other wish-fulfilling trees, a slab of stone much like [the legendary magic stone called] Pandukambalashilatala, and Sudharma, assembly hall of the devas.[24]

In the sky above these, perched upon magnificent clouds, in ascending order are the Yamas, Tushitas, and the other deva-realms,[25] filled with the measureless array of gods and their possessions.

Interspersed between the levels [of deva realms] are the "eight auspicious symbols," including the precious parasol [36] [in the south], the golden fish, the vase, the lotus, the white conch shell with clockwise swirls, the magnificent knot, the banner of victory [37] [in the north] and the golden wheel.[26]

There are the "eight auspicious objects," including the mirror, vermillion dye, the white conch shell, medicine extracted from an elephant's brain, *durva* grass, *bilva* fruit, yoghurt and white mustard seed.[27]

There are also the "seven semi-precious articles" [associated with royalty], including the sleeping-couch, throne, cushion, sword, shoes, snakeskin and robe.

There are the "special substances which prolong life," such as the "six good medicines,"[28] and many other medicinal and nutritious substances; a beautiful vase of *amrita* and other elixirs.

There is the sword [of prajna], the book [*Prajnaparamita*], the

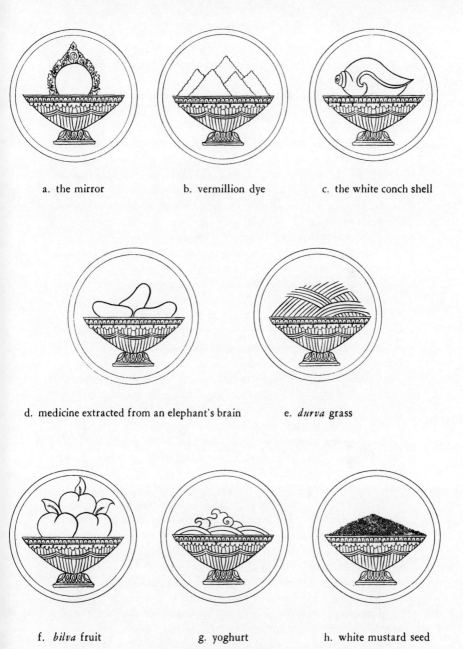

a. the mirror

b. vermillion dye

c. the white conch shell

d. medicine extracted from an elephant's brain

e. *durva* grass

f. *bilva* fruit

g. yoghurt

h. white mustard seed

Fig. 6. The Eight Auspicious Objects.

vina and other musical instruments, and other "articles which bring insight and renown."

There is a rain of rainbow-colored flowers, a pond of perfumed water, a lotus garden, a magical bird and antelope, and other "wonderful offerings."

[As you recite the liturgy,][29] mentally offer all things which gratify the senses of sight, hearing, smell, taste and touch, as well as [things offered by] the servants of gods and goddesses. In brief, imagine that you are offering all the possessions of gods and men that can possibly be accumulated, as well as all the wonderful things in the ten directions which are not owned by anyone.

[Then recite the four-line prayer of offering].[30]

Ten million times one hundred, or a billion worlds like that composed of the four continents, Mt. Meru, etc., comprise a "trichiliocosm." Without reservations, offer countless similar universes to the precious guru. Fill them to the brim with Samantabhadra's clouds of offerings,[31] your body and possessions and those of other sentient beings, your parents, your relatives and all wholesome acts. Then, pray for [universal], unobstructed attainment of enlightenment and the supreme siddhi of Mahamudra in this very lifetime.[32]

[Then, hold up the mandala while you recite the mandala-mantra,[33] and toss a bit of rice into the air as an offering. Then recite the prayer for the achievement of the aims of the Mandala-Offering].[34]

[After offering one mandala of thirty-seven features, sweep the rice off the disk with your right hand. To offer the "short" mandalas, simply] offer the seven piles of rice with your hand while you visualize [the universe] in your mind, and recite the four-line prayer [of offering,[35] once for each construction and visualization] without interruption.

[After offering one "long" mandala], when you are repeating the practice many times [in a session], if your mind cannot cope with the elaborate visualization [described above], at least imagine clearly and in the proper order that you are offering the ground, the iron mountain, Mt. Meru, the four continents and the sun and moon,[36] filling this perfect universe and sky with all the offerings they can possibly hold.

There are many kinds of mandalas, both short and long, ranging [in complexity] from five piles of rice to thirty-seven features. The construction of this particular mandala of thirty-seven features must be learned by means of a "visual transmission."[37] When you are counting your Mandala-Offerings,[38] simply offer mandalas of seven features.

[At the end of a session, recite the prayer for the attainment of Mahamudra,[39] the prayer offering the Seven Branches of Religious Service[40] and the concluding prayer].[41]

Finally, light radiates from the deities visualized on the drubpay mandala to whom you have been offering chodpay mandalas. This light strikes you and all other sentient beings, resulting in universal and complete acquisition of the Two Accumulations.

Imagine that these deities dissolve into light and are absorbed into yourself.

Dedicate the merit.

SIGNS OF SUCCESSFUL PRACTICE

The signs which indicate perfection of the Two Accumulations, such as true realization, meditative experience and dreams, are elucidated in the authoritative treatises of this tradition.

In particular, your thoughts will spontaneously turn to the Dharma. Best of all, you will perform religious acts without effort.

COMMENTARY

True Mahamudra meditation is always accompanied by the gathering of the Accumulations and removal of obscurations. But unless you have previously gathered the Accumulations, you will not experience true meditation.

Very few people have gathered the Accumulations; very few people are "karma-carriers."[42]

Each individual who has begun to practice Dharma and acquired a degree of faith certainly has propensities toward wholesome conduct. However, just as a spark cannot become a flame [if you do not take the time to prepare the fuel], such propensities cannot be awakened in an instant. Until they have been awakened [or transformed into] wholesome conduct, you will experience no realization. The little you do experience will not grow. But if you perform the wholesome deeds [described below], this will create the proper conditions for the awakening of your propensities. As soon as they have been awakened, you will experience a powerful wave of realization.

THE ACCUMULATIONS

THE THREE ACCUMULATIONS AND THE TEN PERFECTIONS

The *Semdrel*[43] texts state that there are Three Accumulations to be acquired. [They consist of the Ten Perfections].[44] Generosity, skillful means and intense longing comprise the Accumulation of Merit. Moral conduct, patience and strenuousness comprise the Accumulation of Moral Conduct. Meditative concentration, insight, the five powers and transcending awareness comprise the Accumulation of Transcending Awareness.

THE TWO ACCUMULATIONS AND THE SIX PERFECTIONS

The sutras hold that there are Two Accumulations. [They consist of the Six Perfections]. Generosity and moral conduct comprise the Accumulation of Merit. Insight comprises the Accumulation of Transcending Awareness. Patience, strenuousness and meditative concentration are included in both [Accumulations].

Meritorious acts performed without the enlightened attitude are not conducive to liberation, only to higher rebirth. [The same acts] performed with the enlightened attitude, are conducive to liberation and lead to Buddhahood.

Furthermore, [meritorious acts] performed with no concern for the "three spheres" of activity"[45] comprise the Unsullied Accumulation, the gathering of which is the principal means of attaining enlightenment.

The Six Perfections

1. Generosity. Generosity is threefold:

(1) "Material generosity" involves giving as much food, clothing, furnishings—even ink and paper—as you can afford. At the very least, give food to a beggar instead of turning him away empty handed. Think about how you will give your body and wealth when in the future you possess a *cakravartin's* realm.

(2) "Giving fearlessness" means curing disease, protecting others from misfortune, directing them out of chasms, escorting them out of danger and removing hindrances to their achievement of siddhi and moral conduct. Truly, practice this type of generosity as much as you can. Protect others from the "four injuries": legal punishment, enemies, thieves and wild animals. Then pray for the ability to save them from the miseries of the three lower realms.

(3) "Giving the Dharma" means that—provided you are competent—you explain those aspects of the Dharma which you feel capable of explaining and which will really help others, now and in the long run. [You should do this] without arrogance or desire for recognition.

If you cannot do this, recite the sutras aloud with the hope that the Dharma will be explained to [all beings], human and non-human.

2. *Moral Conduct.* Moral conduct is threefold:

(1) "Renunciation of harmful action" involves rejection of the ten unwholesome acts which are reprehensible in themselves, and unconditional adherence to the three vows, whose violation is reprehensible by Buddha's decree.

(2) The moral conduct of "gathering wholesome dharmas," includes refusing to be content with just one type of wholesome deed; applying wholesome conduct in the broadest sense; and praying that you accomplish any wholesome acts you have not yet performed.

(3) The moral conduct of "acting for the benefit of sentient beings" means engendering the enlightened attitude and then doing all you can to help others. Vigorously pray that you may accomplish any [helpful deeds] you have not performed. It is not enough to be personally free of wrongdoing.

3. *Patience.* Patience is threefold:

(1) The "ability to bear with indifference any injury inflicted by others," including verbal abuse, beating, striking, robbery or murder.

(2) The "ability to bear difficult circumstances with no concern for your own suffering," such as conditions unsuitable for Dharma practice, illness, pain, hunger, thirst, weariness or fatigue.

(3) The "patience consisting of certainty about the Dharma,"[46] that is, intellectual receptivity which can fearlessly accept such [religious truths] as the profound skillful methods of the Mantrayana, the great and mighty deeds of Buddhas and Bodhisattvas, and the significance of "emptiness which is beyond verbalization."

Meditate with patience!

4. *Strenuousness.* Strenuousness is threefold:

(1) The "strenuousness which constitutes the armor of a Bodhisattva," who delights in wholesome action without timidity. It involves never taking the indifferent attitude that a particular wholesome deed is too insignificant to perform, and never taking the diffident attitude that a particular wholesome deed is beyond your capabilities.

(2) The "strenuousness of application," involves pursuing a constructive undertaking to its completion, without slacking off.

(3) The "strenuousness of refusing to turn back." Once you have begun [a practice], even if the "signs of warmth"[47] and other benefits

do not arise immediately, you do not yield to frustration but practice more and more assiduously until you achieve the results.

Apply strenuousness!

5. *Meditative Concentration.* [Meditative concentration is three-fold]:

(1) The "meditative concentration in which you strictly control your physical and mental acts and remain happy in this life."

(2) The "meditative concentration in which you acquire the positive qualities [of spiritually advanced beings]," including the super-sensible cognitions[48] and the ability to mentally create apparitional beings.[49]

(3) The "meditative concentration in which you benefit sentient beings" by relying on samadhi.

[In order to practice] the three kinds of meditative concentration, you must first achieve a state of flawless tranquility.[50] It is absolutely essential to master this tranquility, since it is the basis for acquisition of all positive qualities.

To achieve a state of tranquility, the mind requires solitude. Mental solitude springs from physical solitude. Physical solitude results from minimizing your goals and activities by having few desires and being content with meager food, clothing and shelter.

In brief, the sources of tranquility [and hence, of all positive qualities] are: (1.) having few desires and (2.) being content.

6. *Insight.* [Insight is threefold]:

(1) The "insight of understanding ultimate reality" by realizing its true nature—openness.

(2) The "insight of understanding relative reality," that is, the inevitability of cause and result and dependent origination.

(3) The "insight of knowing what will benefit others," through applying the "four means of attracting others."[51]

Alternatively, [the three types of insight are]: (1) "insight arising from hearing, (2) from pondering and (3) from meditating."[52]

Achieve all of these as well as you can.

Results of Acquiring the Two Accumulations
by Practicing the Six Perfections

Acquisition of the Accumulations yields the measureless, delightful rewards of godly or human existences. The complete and perfect acquisition of the Two Accumulations and the Six Perfections ultimately results in the attainment of omniscient Buddhahood.

Accumulation of Merit: The Seven Branches of Religious Service

Do not think that your lack of material possessions will prevent you from gathering the Accumulations. It is said that a person who has some faith and insight has an incredible capacity to accumulate merit. If, motivated by the enlightened attitude, you simply offer the Seven Branches of Religious Service,[53] all your obscurations will be destroyed and your Accumulation of Merit will be limitless as the sky.

It is said that a person who performs but one prostration will gain ten benefits:

1. a handsome face
2. a good complexion
3. influential speech
4. influence over associates
5. the affection of gods and men
6. the companionship of holy men
7. robust health
8. wealth
9. higher rebirth
10. liberation

It is also said that a person who performs one prostration with great reverence will be born a *cakravartin* as many times as the number of atoms in the piece of ground over which his five limbs [are extended in full prostration], from the surface down to the golden ground.

It is said that a person who merely folds his hands to the Precious Ones receives ten benefits, including a beautiful form and many attendants.

Numerous rewards of this kind are elucidated in detail in the sutras.

The great Geshes[54] of the Kadampa sect engaged in no other Dharma practice but constant, strenuous application of the Seven Branches of Religious Service. It was the customary practice of the great Kagyudpas, including Nyam-me Dagpo (Gampopa). But nowadays it seems to have all but disappeared.

Today we have no inclination to gather the Accumulations to perfection as we ought to do. Even if we do practice [the Seven Branches]

to some degree, we are so lacking in faith and strenuousness that we
never succeed in gathering the Accumulations. We let our sacred images,
books and stupas collect dust. Some reckless ones even leave them under
dirty rags! We place sooty butter-lamps in offering bowls and on altars,
while showing undue concern for our own physical appearance. Never
do we offer a single flower to the Precious Ones in a spirit of openness
and compassion. It is said that a person who has never recited the [prayer
of the] Seven Branches of Religious Service has accumulated no merit.
Where does merit come from? It comes only from acquisition of the
Accumulations!

If we possess one grain of rice, we eat it if it is edible and offer it
if it is inedible! Even those of us who have gold, silver, silk, horses,
cattle and the like, say "We are so poor in merit that we have nothing
better to offer" and proudly offer a tiny lamp or scrap of food. Thus we
offer lies to the Precious Ones. Do you suppose all this will lead to [the
Accumulation of] Merit?? Hence, it is very important to make offerings
in accordance with your wealth.

In all the sutras and tantras, there is nothing said about gathering
the Accumulations that is more profound than the Seven Branches of
Religious Service. Each branch of the practice yields more merit than
the one preceding it. The merit accumulated by presenting offerings is
greater than that accumulated by performing prostrations; the merit of
confessing is greater than that of presenting offerings; the merit of delighting in wholesome deeds is greater than that of confessing, and so on.

Whether you choose to recite a long or a short version of the "Seven
Branches," it is most important that you ponder the significance [of
what you are reciting]. Mere recitation is a farce.

CONCLUSION

It is said that nothing can be offered with the hands that is more meritorious than this Mandala-Offering. This offering encompasses the practices of the Six Perfections and has the same beneficial results.

The measureless benefits you will enjoy as a result of offering the
mandala are elucidated elsewhere. The *Kutagara sutra*[55] states that merely
building a mandala of the universe gives you dominion over [the actual
universe, including] the four continents and the deva realms. The sutra
implies that merely sprinkling scented water on the mandala and offering
flowers leads to rebirth among the four types of Maharajakayika gods.[56]

In brief, the profound Mandala-Offering is included in these instructions in the Foundations because it is so useful for the rapid perfection of the Accumulations.

However boastful you may be about your generosity, your [ordinary offerings are by their nature] numerically limited to a hundred, a thousand, ten thousand, a hundred thousand, etc. When you offer a gift with the egotistical thought that "I have offered this much" or with desire for recognition, your gift is tainted by these [unwholesome thoughts]. [Ordinary offerings] tend to make us feel hopeful or anxious about whether they will or will not please the guru. Furthermore, recipients [of such offerings are by their nature] numerically limited to a hundred, a thousand and so on.

The Mandala-Offering is the consummate offering because it includes all the riches of the entire universe. It is not susceptible to the taints of proud thoughts, since you think, "I am offering a product of the mind." It does not inspire hope or fear about pleasing [or displeasing] the Precious Ones. A person who [offers the mandala], and visualizes the excellent recipients of the offerings—the Precious Ones in the ten directions and four times[57]—the spacious realms, etc., cannot help but gather the Accumulations with every thought, word and deed. Thus, strive earnestly to do so!

Build new temples and symbols of Buddha's body, speech and mind. Repair old ones. Serve the Sangha. If you have nothing to offer, sweep the shrine room, perform prostrations and circumambulate it as you offer prayers of praise.

To visualize Buddha while joining your palms or tossing a flower into the air [as an offering] is said to yield immeasurable merit. Thus, you who are a recipient of the fortunate and privileged human body—not the inferior body of an animal, who can neither distinguish between wholesome and unwholesome acts, chant a single "Mani" or fulfill a moral obligation—must practice Dharma without delay! Do not let this human life go to waste! No matter how you do so, it is most important that you establish wholesome tendencies of every kind.

NOTES

1. "Mandala" is here the circular disk upon which the drubpay and chodpay mandalas are built.

2. By giving it to monks, the poor or wild birds and animals. (Lama)

3. A mandala is symbolically cleaned by rubbing the "pulse" or inner part of the wrist around its rim thrice clockwise, while reciting the purificatory mantras.

In some traditions it is cleaned counterclockwise, or first clockwise and then counterclockwise. See F. D. Lessing, "Miscellaneous Lamaist Notes I: Notes on the Thanksgiving Offering." *Central Asiatic Journal*, 2, no. 1: 65.

4. Two purificatory mantras. The first removes the imperfections of the materials which comprise the drubpay mandala; the second removes the mandala's substantiality, transforming it to "pure emptiness." It then reappears "out of emptiness" as the palatial abode of the sources of refuge. (Lama)

5. It has four sides, four stories and is made of magnificent materials. (Kalu Rinpoche)

6. See *'Phags-lam*, 111/1–2.

7. The eyes, throat and heart of each of the visualized gurus, yidams, Buddhas, Bodhisattvas and dharmapalas. See chapter 3, n. 9.

8. Any deity is said to exist in two respects: 1. as an "awareness deity" (*ye-shes-pa'i lha*), the "real" deity whose existence does not directly depend on a meditator's visualization; 2. as a "sacred bond deity" (*dam-tshig-pa'i lha*), who exists only for aspirants who have made the sacred commitment (*dam-tshig*) to keep him as a personal yidam. (LPL) Visualizing the merging of these two aspects greatly increases a deity's effectiveness as a source of refuge. (Lama)

9. 1. Flowers, 2. incense, 3. butter-lamp, 4. scented water and 5. food. (Lama)

10. The room, the meditator's body, the mandala disk and the rice must be very clean. (Lama)

11. See Lokesh Chandra and Raghu Vira, eds., *Kalacakra-tantra and Other Texts*. Sata-pitaka series, vol. 69–70. New Delhi: Internat'l. Acad. of Indian Culture, 1966, chap. 1.

This important document reached Tibet in the eleventh century. See G. N. Roerich, transl., *The Blue Annals*, vol. 2. Calcutta: Asiatic Society, 1952, pp. 753–838.

12. It does not matter which of the two tools are used, since the end result of practicing the Foundations is the realization of Mahamudra, which is beyond distinctions. (Lama)

13. See chapter 2, n. 2.

14. According to the Abhidharma, a golden disk, thousands of *yojanas* (1 *yojana* = 9 miles, approx.) deep, supports the earth's surface. A circle of wind 1,600,000 yojanas deep, created ". . . par la force des actes des êtres," supports this. The circle of wind is supported by a circle of water 1,200,000 yojanas deep, created as follows: "Par la souveraineté . . . des actes des êtres, tombe des nuages amoncelés sur le cercle du vent, une pluie dont les gouttes sont comme des timons de char. Cette eau forme le cercle de l'eau . . ." *Kosa*, chap. 3, pp. 45–6; 138–39.

15. This refers to the descriptive liturgy found in *'Phags-lam*, 111/3–112/1, in which each of the thirty-seven main features of the ideal universe is named.

16. An italicized number in square brackets following the name of a feature, indicates the setting of a pile of rice representing that feature upon the mandala disk. Only the thirty-seven main features have been numbered. See fig. 3 for the position of each numbered pile.

17. For example, the blue color of Meru's southern slope gives Jambudvipa, our own continent, its blue color and sky.

18. Nagas: snake-like nature deities. In Buddhist myth they are pictured as extremely intelligent beings inhabiting lake bottoms, where they hoard various treasures. The naga has played an important role in Buddhism. See L. W. Bloss, "The Buddha and the Naga: A Study in Buddhist Folk Religiosity," *History of Religions*, 13, no. 1: 36–53.

19. According to H. Zimmer in *Philosophies of India*, Princeton: Bollingen, 1951, the idea of the *cakravartin* or universal ruler had its roots in pre-Aryan India. As a Buddhist symbol it connotes worldly supremacy, the secular equivalent of the Buddha's spiritual supremacy. The *cakravartin* bears the same "major and minor marks of perfection" as the Buddha.

The "seven possessions" are symbols associated with this worldly supremacy, the central one being the wheel or cakra. "The day when this first appeared to him . . . it stood as the sign that he was to undertake the campaign of unifying the whole earthly realm. He rose and followed the symbol, which now moves before him as he marches." (Zimmer, *Philosophies*, p. 129.)

According to Kalu Rinpoche, propelled by the monarch's great stock of merit, the wheel efficiently transports himself and his entire retinue to their desired destination as they ride on its huge hub. The wish-fulfilling gem not only takes care of the *cakravartin's* own desires but grants the wishes of all who stand within the range of its great radiance.

Each of the remaining possessions is the best of its class and brings happiness, peace and prosperity to the *cakravartin* and his realm. See Zimmer, *Philosophies*, pp. 127–39.

20. Legs, head, tail and trunk.

21. *rdorje-khu-tshur*. With closed fists resting on hips. (Lama)

22. Indian stringed instrument resembling the lute.

23. The sun, whose nature is the element fire, looks like a clear lens through which hot rays are being focused. The moon, whose nature is the element water, looks like a lens of frosted glass, cool and soothing to the eyes. (Lama)

24. Vishnu's city, on top of Mt. Meru, is inhabited by gods. The walls of the city surround Indra's palace in the manner of a chilkor (see chap 3, n. 20). The palace is square and multi-storied, each story slightly narrower than the one below.

Pariyatra is the wish-fulfilling tree whose roots are in the asura realm, but whose leaves, fruit and flowers grace only the deva realm. This predicament is the cause of continual strife between devas and asuras.

The magic white stone (Tib. Ar-mo-ni-ka or A-mo-li-ka) was that on which the Buddha's mother sat as he preached the Dharma to her in the deva realm. (LPL) It was also the relic Milarepa left for his disciples. See W. Y. Evans-Wentz, *Tibet's Great Yogi Milarepa*. New York: Oxford, 1957, p. 301.

The above features are visualized, but not represented in the rice mandala.

25. For these, see *Kosa,* chap. 3. pp. 159–74.

26. Of the eight symbols, only two—the parasol and the banner of victory—are mentioned in the liturgy. Placing the two piles of rice representing them on the disk completes the mandala construction. The remaining auspicious symbols and the rest of the offerings are simply visualized here and there in the sky above the mandala-universe.

27. These eight are considered auspicious in Indian culture. The Buddhists connect them with episodes in Shakyamuni's life. (LPL) For example, when he rejected extreme asceticism, his first meal included yoghurt. When he attained enlightenment, he was sitting on a bunch of *durva* or *kusha* grass under the Bo tree.

28. *bzang-po drug*: six medicinal roots used for digestive ailments. They are grown in India and were imported into Tibet. (LPL)

29. See *'Phags-lam,* 111/3–112/1.

30. See *'Phags-lam,* 112/5–6.

31. This is a reference to a passage in the *Gandavyuha sutra,* in which the Bodhisattva Samantabhadra mentally creates an inexhaustable flow of wondrous gifts and offers it to all the Buddhas. See G. C. C. Chang, *Buddhist Teaching of Totality.* Pittsburgh: Penn. State, 1971, p. 187, 190.

32. See *'Phags-lam,* 112/2–3.

33. See *'Phags-lam,* 112/4.

34. See *'Phags-lam,* 112/4–5. This recitation completes one offering of the "long" mandala of thirty-seven features. This "long" offering must be performed only once per session. Further offerings in the same session may consist of "short" mandalas of seven features.

35. Same as n. 30, above.

36. According to Kalu Rinpoche, even while building "short" mandalas and reciting the four-line prayer, one should try to visualize the mandala of thirty-seven features.

37. Demonstration of the mandala's construction by a guru or trained fellow Buddhist. (LPL)

38. I.e., in a regular practice session.

39. See *'Phags-lam,* 112/6–7.

40. See *'Phags-lam,* 112/7. The Seven Branches are:
   1. performing prostrations
   2. presenting offerings
   3. confessing harmful deeds
   4. delighting in wholesome deeds
   5. urging teachers to preach the Dharma
   6. urging enlightened ones not to pass into nirvana
   7. dedicating all the merit you have earned to the enlightenment of all.

Practicing the Seven Branches accomplishes the Accumulation of Merit. (Lama) See pp. 109–110 for details.

41. See *'Phags-lam,* 112/7–113/1.

42. "(Good) karma-carrier" (*las-'phro*): one who has a tendency to do good deeds.

43. *Byang-chub-sems-kyi'grel-ba; Bodhicittavivarana. bsTan.*, P. 2665–2666: Nagarjuna's commentaries on the ten stages of Bodhisattva-hood. This scheme of three instead of two Accumulations is very uncommon and is not used again in this text. (LPL)

44. The Perfections not included in the more common group of six are four higher achievements attained only by Bodhisattvas, who: 1. apply skillful means on a universal basis; 2. generate intense longing to reach enlightenment and liberate others; 3. apply the five powers: confidence, strenuousness, inspection (*dran-pa;* Skt. *smriti*), meditative concentration and insight; 4. possess transcending awareness. (LPL)

For details on the Ten Perfections, see H. V. Guenther's *Jewel Ornament,* pp. 239–56.

45. *'khor-gsum yongs-dag;* Skt. *trimandala-parishuddha*: seems to be synonymous with *'khor-gsum dmigs-med,* chapter 3, n. 23.

46. Intellectual openness characteristic of a Mahayana type of person. This gives him the impetus to undertake meditation aimed at firsthand discovery of meaning in religious "truths" proclaimed by his teachers or in scriptures. A person with a Hinayana attitude, on the other hand, feels threatened by "emptiness" and other "truths" he cannot immediately apprehend, and closes his mind to them. (Lama; LPL)

Here, "Hinayana" and "Mahayana" denote attitudes, not sects.

The three kinds of patience overcome the three kinds of obstacles to religious practice: the first defeats "outer" or environmental obstacles; the second, "inner" obstacles such as illness or wandering thoughts; the third, "secret" obstacles such as doubt or non-belief. (Lama)

47. *drod-rtags*: sensations, similar to those experienced when blessing is received, which indicate that meditation is having some effect. Some meditators vow to remain in solitude until such signs occur. (Lama)

48. See chapter 1, n. 17.

49. *rdzu-'phrul;* Skt. *riddhi*: ability to create benevolent apparitions, such as forms of Buddhas. Often contrasted with *cho-'phrul;* Skt. *pratiharya*: ability to create demonic apparitions. (Lama)

50. *zhi-gnas;* Skt. *shamatha*: tranquility achieved by withdrawing attention from the chaos of physical and mental stimuli. Techniques include concentrating on a single object and "watching" one's breathing. Prescribed, by this tradition, as a prerequisite for other meditative practice.

51. "Four means of attracting others": techniques by which a Buddha, Bodhisattva or skilled religious teacher attracts others to himself, and hence to the religious life. The first three are: 1. generosity; 2. kind words; 3. helpfulness. The fourth (*'jig-rten don mthun-pa;* Skt. *samanarthata*) is interpreted by Edgerton and others as a teacher's adoption of identical religious aims for himself and others. But according to the Lama, it refers to his conformity with local customs to avoid alienating others.

52. Wayman explains these three stages of insight as follows:
One who has faith and endures the hardship to hear the teaching

has the first level of insight . . . the insight consisting of hearing. . . .
The second stage, the insight consisting of pondering . . . should involve the laid-down procedure of Buddhist meditation. . . . Having
heard with faith and pondered again and again . . . the third stage
[is] putting that teaching into practice, the insight of cultivating one's
life. *Buddhist Tantras*, p. 61.

53. See n. 40, above.

54. Here, "Geshe" denotes a Lama, usually of the Kadampa or Gelugpa sect, possessing certain extensive scholarly credentials.

55. *Khang-bu brtsegs-pa'i mdo. bKa'.*, P. 998.

56. Highest class of gods in the Desire realm.

57. Past, present, future and timelessness. (LPL)

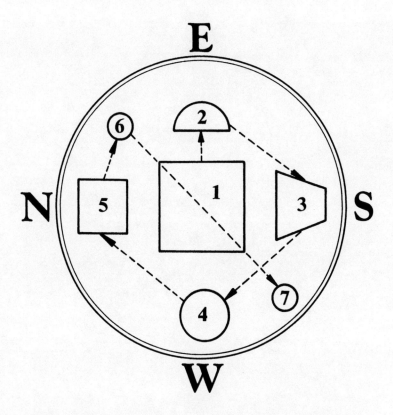

Fig. 7. Diagram of the Mandala of the Universe of seven features, for construction.

Fig. 8. Vajravarahi.

5 FOURTH OF THE FOUR SPECIAL FOUNDATIONS

The Guru-Yoga Which Rapidly Confers Blessing

[Having successfully completed the stages of commitment, purification and enrichment (i.e., the three previous Foundations), the aspirant is almost ready to begin the Mahamudra practices. He lacks only two prerequisites:

1. Authorization and ability to do these practices. This can only be conferred by a guru who has himself received them.

2. A closer relationship with this guru and symbolic admission to his lineage.

Receipt of these two comprises the "blessing" promised to one who practices the Guru-Yoga. Hence, this ritual is the final Foundation for Mahamudra practice.

Since the ritual involves receiving the Four Empowerments from the guru visualized as the Buddha Vajradhara, the aspirant should have an unshakable conviction that his guru really is the Buddha. Kongtrul appreciates the fact that this conviction will have to be gradually developed and provides numerous techniques for doing so.

Practice of the Guru-Yoga involves:

1. Sitting cross-legged and reciting a purificatory mantra.

2. Visualizing yourself as Vajravarahi (Dorje Phamo).

3. Visualizing Vajradhara while thinking of him as your root-guru seated on the crown of your head, surrounded by various gurus and other sources of refuge, and chanting the descriptive liturgy.

4. Praying to them.

5. Reciting the prayer of the Seven Branches of Religious Service while imagining that you are actually performing them.

6. Praying for realization of the three Buddha-kayas.

7. Reciting the long prayer to the gurus of the Mahamudra lineage.

8. Reciting the short prayer to the gurus of the Mahamudra lineage.

9. Praying to the gurus for various blessings.

10. Reciting the "Ma-nam Four" three times, and the invocation of the Karmapa several times.

11. Reciting the six-line prayer for blessings the desired number of times for the session.

12. Praying to the guru for the Four Empowerments; visualizing your receipt of the Empowerments and the results of this.

13. Visualizing the guru dissolving into light and then into yourself.

14. Letting your mind rest.

15. Dedicating merit.

To complete the Guru-Yoga, the six-line prayer must be recited a total of 111,111 times.]

MEDITATION

Meditate that everything is "purified to emptiness" by means of the *svabhava mantra*.[1] You now emerge out of emptiness, looking like Vajra-varahi (Dorje Phamo) and standing on a corpse, red lotus and sun.[2]

As you have not yet purified all your obscurations, performing the Guru-Yoga as your ordinary self would not net you any blessing. But performing it as the yidam will facilitate quick and easy receipt of bless-ing. Thus, [when practicing the Guru-Yoga], you should focus your attention on the yidam who appeals to you.

Vajravarahi is the mother who begat all Buddhas. She is essentially Mahamudra, appearing in the form of Sahaja. She belongs to a family of yoginis who are especially warm-hearted toward sentient beings. Hence, through her, blessing may be quickly received. It is especially propitious [to visualize yourself as Vajravarahi while you practice this meditation] since she was the secret yidam[3] of Lords Marpa, Mila and Dagpo. Do as they did!

[Begin by reciting the liturgy[4] which describes the following:]

On the crown of your head, or in the sky before you, sits your own root-guru as he appeared in Taking Refuge. He is the essence of all Buddhas of the three times. In the form of Vajradhara, he sits on a lotus and moon seat atop a jewelled throne upheld by eight lions and covered with priceless silks.

The Kagyudpa gurus are seated [on his head] in a column extend-ing from your root-guru [as Vajradhara] up to Vajradhara himself. This column is surrounded by gurus of the Drikhung, Drugpa, Tshalpa and Talung [branches of the Kagyud sect], and by other gurus of the medita-tive tradition[5]—a veritable ocean of siddhas! They are surrounded by the clouds of gurus who transmitted the Great Perfection, Six Yogas, Path and Result and Shijay Chodyul;[6] and the gurus of the tradition of in-tellectual discipline.[7]

Think that the *damtshig* and *yeshe* aspect[8] of each of the yidams,

Buddhas, Bodhisattvas, dakas, dakinis and dharmapalas who surround the gurus, have been primordially inseparable.

With deep sincerity and longing, clearly recite [the prayer to Vajradhara and the other sources of refuge] which begins, "Enlightened Lord . . ."⁹

Then recite the prayer for the Seven Branches of Religious Service which begins, "To you who have come from the highest Buddharealm . . ."¹⁰ and the prayer [for realization of the three Buddha-kayas].¹¹

Now recite the long and short prayers¹² to the gurus of the Mahamudra lineage. [First, recite the long prayer¹³ which ends with the prayer for realization of Mahamudra.]¹⁴

[Then recite the short prayer and pray for blessings].¹⁵

[Recite the prayers indicated below each time you practice the meditation:]

First recite the "Ma-nam Four"¹⁶ [at least three times].

Recite the vajra-invocation of the great Lord Dusum Khyenpa¹⁷ [one hundred times or more].

Recite the six-line prayer for blessings¹⁸ repeatedly, without allowing your thoughts to stray.

Recite the prayer for the Four Empowerments which begins, "Glorious, holy gurus . . ."¹⁹

After you recite [the first verse], the deities surrounding [the gurus of the lineage] dissolve into light. This light is absorbed into the gurus of the lineage. The gurus of the lineage gradually melt into one another, dissolve into light and then into the form of your root-guru.

Then, from the forehead [of your root-guru], who is essentially all the Precious Ones combined, white light radiates. It is absorbed into the space between your eyebrows, and removes your physical obscurations, such as the taking of life and other [physical misdeeds you have committed in the past]. You have received the Vase Empowerment.²⁰ You are now able to begin the meditation of the Developing Stage.²¹ As a result, you become a fortunate one, a Nirmanakaya.

In the same way as before, red light radiates from the guru's throat. It dissolves into your own throat, removing verbal obscurations such as lies [which you have told in the past]. You have received the Secret Empowerment. You are now able to practice Tsa-Lung²² meditation. Thus, you are a fortunate one, a Sambhogakaya.

From the guru's heart, blue light radiates and is absorbed into your own heart. It removes your mental obscurations, such as perverted views. You have received the Empowerment of Insight and Transcending

Awareness. You are now able to practice Nyom-jug[23] meditation through which you become a fortunate one, a Dharmakaya.

From the three places [on the guru's body], white, red and blue light radiates and is absorbed into your forehead, throat and heart. It removes your mental, emotional and meditation-clinging obscurations[24] which obscure the three gates.[25] You have received the Fourth Empowerment. You are able to practice Mahamudra,[26] the meditation of the non-separateness of awareness and emptiness. This makes you a fortunate one, a Svabhavikakaya.

Once more, delighted by your fervent devotion and reverence, your guru, smiling cheerfully, dissolves into light.[27] This light enters through the crown of your head and is absorbed into your heart region. Think that the guru's mind and your own mind have become inseparable, and let your mind rest for as long as possible unobstructed by conceptualization, just as it is in its natural state.

As soon as you emerge from this non-conceptual state, think that all appearances are the various forms of your guru. All sounds are his speech which is devoid of sound-of-its-own. All thoughts which arise and dart to and fro are spontaneous manifestations of his vajra-awareness.

Dedicate the merit.

HOW TO KEEP UP THE PRACTICE BETWEEN MEDITATION SESSIONS

Even between meditation sessions, when you are walking, imagine yourself to be circumambulating the guru seated on a lotus and moon in the right-hand quarter of the sky. When you are eating and drinking, imagine yourself to be offering your food and drink—which has melted into *amrita*—to the guru seated in a red lotus at your throat. Meditate that all your speech is prayer, that all your activities, even walking and sitting, constitute service to the guru.

As you fall asleep try to visualize the form of your guru—about the size of your finger—seated at your heart. Light radiates from him and fills your body and room. When you awaken, imagine that the guru is seated on the crown of your head, and pray to him with faith and reverence. Do this whenever you are sitting.

As soon as you finish building a new house, making new clothes and so on, offer them to the guru either actually or mentally.

When illness strikes, imagine that *amrita* flows down from the tiny form of the guru, seated at the afflicted part of your body, and clears away the disease. Happily meditate that all methods of curing illness, bad deeds and obscurations have sprung from the guru's blessing. Even when a demonic apparition appears, imagine it to be the play of the guru's Buddha-activity urging you on toward wholesome conduct.

In brief, imagine all pleasant experiences to be the guru's blessing. Meditate that all painful experiences are the guru's compassion.[28] It is essential that you make use of such experiences to enhance your devotion and reverence and do not look elsewhere for a remedy [for suffering].[29]

COMMENTARY

IMPORTANCE OF RECEIVING THE GURU'S BLESSING

Now, understand the following:

In general, in order to follow the Mantrayana or Vajrayana, especially to receive instructions in the meditation of the Fulfillment Stage, you must first receive the guru's blessing. Until you have received it, you will not be on the true path.

It is said that a disciple who is intensely devoted and reverent toward a fully qualified Vajrayana master[30] with whom he has formed a sacred bond will achieve supreme and worldly siddhi without doing anything else. But a person who lacks devotion and reverence for the guru, even if he performs a great many Nyendrub practices[31] for the yidams of the four tantras, will obtain no supreme siddhi whatsoever.

As for worldly siddhi, he will not achieve long life, wealth, power, etc., no matter how hard he may strive. Anything he does achieve will have been won through great hardship. This is the "non-profound path."[32]

On the other hand, if he develops true devotion and reverence, all obstacles will be cleared, uprooted and expelled from his path, and he will obtain supreme and worldly siddhi by this method alone. Therefore, we call it the "profound path of the Guru-Yoga."

POSITIVE AND NEGATIVE QUALITIES OF A MASTER AND DISCIPLE

A master or disciple who has such serious defects as to lack compassion, to be easily angered, to be malicious, spiteful, or proud; to be very attached to his money, property, relatives, etc.; to be undisciplined in words or deeds or full of self-praise, should be rejected.

In particular, you should absolutely avoid [a master who commits the following misdeeds], for such a master can only confer the "blessing" of Mara:

1. Explaining or demonstrating to a crowd of common folk [such practices as] Tsa-Lung or Mahamudra meditation, those which employ mantras, or the essentials of the profound Fulfillment Stage;

2. [Boastfully claiming to possess] instructions others lack and spreading instructions in the profound philosophy and practice of the Mantrayana in the marketplace;

3. Behaving in an undisciplined manner;

4. Verbalizing the ultimate philosophical perspective;[33]

5. Greatly coveting money or property belonging to the Precious Ones;

6. Being highly deceitful and hypocritical;

7. Giving empowerments and instructions which do not belong to any tradition;

8. Indulging in the pleasures of liquor and sex;

9. Teaching a doctrine which conflicts with the Dharma, in words of his own invention, because he does not know how to teach the true path.

A master should not form a close relationship with a disciple who lacks faith, violates his sacred commitments, flatters new acquaintances, is very restless and so on, unless the disciple gradually improves.

The characteristics of a guru are discussed at length in the sutras and tantras. A guru should not let his faith or sacred commitments deteriorate, should perform a great deal of Nyendrub and know the practices well, should care little for the eight worldly dharmas[34] and should personally practice any teachings before he explains them to others.

At the very least, a disciple should have faith, should be capable of keeping sacred commitments and should always avoid harmful companions.

THE GURU-DISCIPLE RELATIONSHIP

Before you have requested Dharma instruction or empowerment from a master, examine his qualities. But once you have received [any instruction or empowerment] from him, even if he flaunts the four immoral acts,[35] you may not turn your faith away from him, slander him, examine his qualities or do anything but treat him as one worthy of devotion and reverence.

It is said:

> Once you have listened to a single brief discourse,
> If you lack respect for your guru,
> You will be born a dog one hundred times,
> And a butcher after that.

In these times, it is impossible to find a guru who has rid himself of all defects and perfected positive qualities. Even if it were possible to find such a guru, without pure vision you could mistake his positive qualities for faults, just as Devadatta[36] saw faults in the Bhagavan.

Since most people today are "rich" in nothing but bad deeds, we often see positive qualities as faults, and faults as positive qualities. Since we often regard those who can neither demonstrate nor preserve religious qualities as "worthy ones,"[37] it is difficult for us to really know anyone's qualities by examination.

Just as a tsa-tsa's[38] shape is determined by the mould from which it is made, a guru—particularly a Mahamudra teacher—who has achieved no realization is incapable of bringing his disciple to the pinnacle of realization.[39] After you receive the transmission[40] of the lineage of Nyam-me Dagpo, Lord Dusum Khyenpa, Shang-tshalpa, God-tsangpa or another [Mahamudra master], think of the master in whom you have the greatest faith as your root-guru, and pray to him. If you do this, you will receive the blessing. This has been promised!

Since Buddha prophesied that the great Nyam-me Dagpo would spread the Mahamudra teachings, it is particularly important for one who is interested in practicing Mahamudra to place his faith in Jetsun Gampopa. Furthermore, he should meditate on the non-separateness of [Gampopa] and his own root-guru.[41] If he regards as his root-guru anyone who has received the blessing of the lineage as from father[42] to son, he will find this satisfactory. He will not need to examine his guru's qualities.[43]

Such examination is unnecessary even with respect to other Kagyudpas. All the gurus of the past—the great ones who received the transmission—transferred their realization, their ultimate awareness, to their disciples. Thus, all these gurus have the capacity to bless others.

Even if you do not hear the Dharma directly from a guru as famous as those "fathers and sons," regard any guru who has achieved realization as your root-guru, and you will receive the blessing.

In reality, your guru may be an ordinary being or a manifestation of a Buddha or Bodhisattva. But if you can pray to him while meditating that he is the Buddha, all the Buddhas, Bodhisattvas and yidams will enter the body, speech and mind of your Vajrayana master and work for the benefit of all beings.

According to the *Mukhagama* of Manjushri:[44]

> All those who have contempt for a future Vajradhara
> Have contempt for me; hence, I abandon them.

And further:

> It is I who dwell in the guru's body,
> I who receive offerings from aspirants.
> They please me, thus their karmic obscurations are removed![45]

Thus, to please your root-guru is to please all the Buddhas. Mistreating him is like mistreating all the Buddhas. Presenting offerings to him earns the merit of presenting offerings to all the Buddhas and removes obscurations.

Many sutras and shastras say that our attainment of siddhi is entirely dependent on the guru, and that immeasurable benefits will accrue through our devotion, reverence and presentation of offerings to him.

In the tantras it is said:

> A hundred thousand visualizations of a deity's form,
>   performed a hundred thousand times,
> Are no match for one unwavering visualization
>   of the guru's form.
> A hundred billion Nyendrub practices,
>   performed a hundred thousand times,
> Are not as potent as a prayer to the guru,
>   sincerely offered thrice.
> One who performs a kalpa-worth of Fulfillment Stage meditation,
>   and does this twenty thousand times,
> Is no match for one within whose mind
>   the guru but appears.

From the *Pradipodyotana*:[46]

Oh, son of good family, the merit earned by worshiping one pore on the master's body is greater than the heap of merit earned by worshiping the vajra-body, speech and mind of all the Buddha Bhagavans in the ten directions.

If you ask "Why is this so?", Oh son of good family, the enlightened attitude [possessed by the master] is the very core of the transcending awareness of all Buddhas!

Generally speaking, there is no difference between your relationship with a guru from whom you have heard the sutras of the Hinayana and Mahayana and one from whom you received the transmissions and instructions of the Mantrayana tantras. The only difference is that your relationship with the latter is of greater consequence[47] than your relationship with the former.

Whether a guru is said to be the object of your commission of the first transgression[48] or not, and whether the sacred bond between you is said to be broken or not, depends on you. It does not depend on whether the guru is or is not your root-guru.

As soon as you ask a guru for Mantrayana empowerment, a religious connection exists between you. You must not commit the first transgression against such a guru. Hence, as soon as you ask a guru for any Sutra- or Mantrayana teaching, it is very important that you avoid bad conduct. Although the gurus of the lineage are not your root-gurus and there is no religious connection between you, they too must never be the objects of slander or any other transgression.

In general, do not examine the faults of sentient beings. Knowing that they are your mothers, think of them with gratitude, benevolence and compassion. In particular, do not examine the faults of those who have entered the Dharma's door. Knowing that you are all "in the same boat,"[49] concentrate on their positive qualities and cultivate sympathetic joy, devotion and reverence for them. But especially, do not examine the faults of your guru. From the *Arya-Shraddhabaladhanavataramudra sutra*:[50]

It is a much worse offense to slander a single Bodhisattva[51] than to steal all the possessions of all the sentient beings in this trichiliocosm and destroy all the stupas.

One who belittles and criticizes a Bodhisattva, regardless of the circumstances, will be born in the Howling Hell.[52] His body will be five hundred *yojanas* high and will have five hundred heads, and five hundred ploughs will slice into each of his tongues!

In general, it is an incalculably great offense to slander worthy ones, in particular, Bodhisattvas, but most of all, important persons such as Mantrayana yogins. Furthermore, we do not know who may be a worthy one or a Buddhist yogin. It is said that only a Perfect Buddha can accurately perceive the spiritual capacities of other individuals. Thus, hurling abuse at anyone sweeps away your own positive qualities. Examining the faults of others is the very source of your own ruin. You must look for faults in yourself alone!

Those who lack faith in the guru, even when he is present, and who do not regard religious practitioners as pure will inevitably encounter what they least desire. Others will see them as enemies. They will die in unpleasant circumstances. They will suffer unfavorable death-omens. They will be everyone's target of abuse.

Those who reverently rely on the guru and regard all others as pure will effortlessly gain happiness and renown. They will be praised by all. They will die in pleasant circumstances, see and hear auspicious death-omens, etc.

The great Kagyudpas have said:

If you see your guru as a Buddha you will receive a Buddha's blessing. If you see him as a Bodhisattva, you will receive a Bodhisattva's blessing. If you see him as a siddha you will receive a siddha's blessing. If you see him as an ordinary person—a good spiritual friend—such is the blessing you will receive. If you feel no devotion or reverence for him, you will receive absolutely no blessing.

There is no Buddha anywhere who is other than your root-guru. He is the unity of all the Precious Ones in the ten directions and three times. All the limitless positive qualities of the Precious Ones are the creative manifestations of the root-guru. Furthermore, everyone everywhere who works for the welfare of sentient beings, as well as the sun, moon, elixirs, medicines, boats and bridges—all these are the guru's creative manifestations!

FOUR THOUGHTS TO BE INSTILLED

1. Think of anyone who has given you empowerments, transmissions, instructions or even reading skills, as an aspect of your root-guru's form. In brief, *resolve that he is a Buddha.*

2. The Buddhas, yidams, and great Kagyud gurus are wonderful indeed. But you have not been taught by them directly; you have not heard them speak. Even if you should meet them, there is nothing for them to do beyond that which your guru has done. Countless Buddhas of

the past have entered nirvana; countless Buddhas of the present reside in the ten directions. Innumerable Buddhas, Bodhisattvas, gurus and yidams exist. However, you have not been fortunate enough to meet a single one of them, even in a dream! But your own root-guru is teaching you the complete, unerring way to achieve Buddhahood in one body, in one lifetime! Surely, though you died trying, *you could not possibly repay his kindness!*

3. When the guru takes an interest in you and gives you religious teachings and gifts, you think about him. When he is far away, you forget about him. When subject to illness or unpleasant events, you think about him. You do not think about him when you are happy. This is no way to behave! Moving, walking, sleeping, sitting, happy or miserable, *continuously think about nothing but the guru!*

4. It is not proper to simply think of the guru once in a while and to recite, "I take refuge," or count your occasional prayers to him. Pray to him with your hair standing on end and tears of great yearning streaming down your face. Your mind will become clear, ordinary appearances will cease and meditative experience will arise without effort. *This is the force of great yearning.*

When these four have been consolidated, you will receive the guru's blessing. Then you will truly possess devotion and reverence which can bring on sudden realization.

The key to the rapid receipt of blessing is meditation on the guru as the Buddha. Moreover, if you are practicing Mahamudra meditation, think of the guru as the unadorned Dharmakaya.[53] If you want a long life, think of him as Amitayus or white Tara.[54] If you wish to cure a disease, think of him as Bhaishajyaguru.[55] He is the foe of all demons. Regard him as inseparable from the Principal One of any tantric mandala on which you are meditating. Thus, he is the "Lord of the Mandala."[56]

CONCLUSION

If you apply the foregoing instructions, you will truly be practicing the Guru-Yoga.

Failure to appreciate the guru's kindness reveals lack of esteem for the Dharma. If you lack such esteem, all your Dharma practice will be futile and will net you no positive qualities no matter how hard you try. If, due to this lack of esteem, you take the arrogant view that it is impossible for the guru to acquire positive qualities, or you take the diffident view that it is impossible for the rest of us to do so, you are meditating with a perverted attitude. Since you have fallen into the first transgression, all your previously accumulated merit is swept away! Respect for the guru and the Dharma will arise of their own accord if you appreciate the guru's kindness. All positive qualities will then be yours spontaneously, with no effort on your part.

If true feelings of devotion and reverence do not come easily to you, make offerings to the Precious Ones, serve the Sangha, and do all the physical and verbal wholesome deeds you can. It is said that if after doing this you meditate and pray: "May any merit I have gathered inspire strong feelings of devotion and reverence," these feelings will definitely arise. A person of great devotion and reverence performs great wholesome acts. One of average devotion and reverence performs average wholesome acts. One of minimal devotion and reverence performs minimal wholesome acts.

Naropa, Maitripa, Mila, Jayulpa[57] and others obtained siddhi solely by undergoing hardships for the sake of their gurus. We are not capable of doing what they did. Uncontrived devotion and reverence do not come easily, but they may gradually be learned with the guidance of prayer.

THE DEVOTIONAL PATH

These are the four branches of the devotional path:

1. DO NOT FIND FAULT WITH THE GURU.

Buddhajnanapada's[58] faithless perception caused him to see Manjushri as a married monk with children. This perception obstructed his attainment of supreme siddhi. Similarly, your own mental attitude causes you to see faults in the guru. How can a Buddha have faults? Whatever he does, let him do it! Even if you see your guru having sexual relations, telling lies and so on, calmly meditate as follows: "These are my guru's unsurpassed skillful methods of training disciples. Through these methods he has brought many sentient beings to spiritual maturity and liberation. This is a hundred, a thousand times more wonderful than preserving a pure moral code! This is not deception or hypocrisy but the highest mode of conduct!"

In particular, when he scolds you, think: "He is destroying my bad deeds!" When he hits you, think: "He is chasing away the demons who obstruct [my spiritual progress]!"

Above all, consider the fact that your guru loves you like a father loves his son. His friendship is always sincere. He is very kind. If he seems displeased or indifferent toward you, think that this is the retribution which will remove your remaining karmic obscurations. Try to please the guru by serving him in all ways possible.

In brief, do not find fault with the guru.

2. APPRECIATE THE POSITIVE ASPECTS OF ALL HIS DEEDS.

From the sayings of the great Kagyudpas:

> Everything this precious perfect guru does,
> No matter what it is, is good.
> All his deeds are excellent.
> In his hands a butcher's evil work
> Is good, and benefits the beasts,
> Inspired by compassion for them all.
>
> When he unites in sex improperly,
> His qualities increase, and fresh arise,
> A sign that means and insight have been joined.
>
> His lies by which we are deceived
> Are just the skillful signs with which
> He guides us on the freedom path.
>
> When he steals, the stolen goods
> Are changed into necessities
> To ease the poverty of all.
>
> When such a guru scolds,
> His words are forceful mantras
> To remove distress and obstacles.
>
> His beatings are blessings,
> Which yield both siddhis,
> And gladden all devout and reverent men.

As it is said above, appreciate the positive aspects of all his deeds.

3. THE ONLY THING TO DO IS CULTIVATE DEVOTION AND REVERENCE, FREE OF EXPECTATION AND ANXIETY.[59]

Meditate on the guru with devotion and reverence and with no concern for whether your acts will please or displease him. Do not expect to achieve supreme siddhi; do not fear [that you will not achieve it]. Whether or not you are embraced by his compassion, whether or not you achieve siddhi, simply cultivate devotion and reverence free of expectation and anxiety.

4. ALWAYS THINK OF YOUR GURU WITH AFFECTION.

A layman of the highest caliber always does his best to help his master in private, public and in between. Such a man is a "this-life-person," [one who is concerned only with what may happen in the next] few months or years.

[A religious person's concerns are long-term]. Until we reach enlightenment, all our hopes and dreams depend on our guru. Any degree of happiness or prosperity we find in this life, future lives and in the bardo, is nothing but the guru's kindness.

Since your acquisition of religious qualities depends solely on the guru, think of all your physical, verbal and mental acts as service to him. Always think of your guru with affection and pray for his long life and the expansion of his good deeds and religious activities.

If you rely on your guru with these attitudes, you will definitely achieve liberation.

The practice of [the path of devotion] is totally encompassed by the following two directives:

1. Do whatever your guru tells you to do.
2. Do whatever your guru wants you to do.

With your body, do prostrations and circumambulations, write, sew, run errands, fetch water and sweep up.

With your speech, offer prayers and praise him. Make your guru's qualities known to others. Ask him what he would like you to do, in gentle, polite and straightforward language. Whether in public or private, do not speak even one word of slander.

In your mind, cultivate only devotion, reverence and pure perception,[60] untainted by a single perverted view. If inappropriate thoughts arise due to bad karma, stop them immediately, and never express them through words or deeds.

If, due to past misdeeds, you go against his wishes, confess sincerely and offer him your body and possessions. Recite the hundred-syllable mantra [of Vajrasattva], propitiatory prayers and confessions. You must not enjoy a morsel of food or speak a friendly word with anyone who goes against the guru's wishes. It is said that if you befriend a man who has contempt for your guru this is just as bad as if you yourself felt such contempt, even though you do not.

You should not be stingy. You should give your guru anything of yours which is valuable or pleasing to him. But you don't do this. If you have valuable goods—fine, expensive things such as young horses, cattle and so on—you keep them for yourself! You offer your worst possessions to the guru and tell him how wonderful you are! You ask him for any empowerments and teachings you desire, no matter how profound they are. If he does not comply, you look at him sadly and say, "But I have been so kind to you!"

Instead of feeling gratitude toward this guru, who has given you Dharma teaching and instructions, you say, "I have done him a great favor by asking him for instruction and listening to him!"

If you are unaware of the fact that it is for your own good that you give offerings and service to the guru, if you present your offerings with pride and self-satisfaction, it would have been better to have made no offering in the first place!

SIGNS OF SUCCESSFUL PRACTICE

The authoritative treatises of this tradition elucidate the nature of the signs—such as true realization, meditative experience and dreams—which indicate that, because you have developed true devotion and reverence, you have received the blessing. In particular, the eight worldly dharmas no longer seem attractive, and your mind is detached from the concerns of this life.

The best signs are the glimpses of realization you experience after your awareness is stripped down to unadorned clarity and openness.

Since your ability to practice Mahamudra, the actual ground-meditation, depends on your receipt of the blessing, it is said:

Do not run full tilt at tranquility and insight. First, cultivate a fertile ground for positive qualities within yourself.

NOTES

1. Recite "Oṁ Svabhāva Shuddha Sarva Dharma Svabhāva Shuddho Haṁ," as in the Mandala practice, and then visualize everything dissolving into emptiness. (Lama)
2. Vajravarahi (Dorje Phamo) is the chief female yidam of the Kagyud sect.
3. A secret yidam is one whose identity is not revealed to others, thus increasing the blessing received by the meditator. (Kalu Rinpoche)
4. See *'Phags-lam*, 113/1–2.

5. *sgrub-brgyud*: used to characterize the Kagyud and Nyingma sects. (LPL)

6. The Great Perfection, Six Yogas, and Path and Result are key practices of the Nyingma, Kagyud and Sakya sects respectively. Shijay Chodyul (*zhi-byed gcod-yul*) or "Chod" was taken to Tibet from India by Phadampa (11th cent.). It became the central practice of the Shijaypa (Zhi-byed-pa) sect which died out when the practice was adopted by all the major sects.

The Chod ritual entails symbolic severence of the pernicious belief in a self. (LPL) For an eyewitness account of the ritual, see A. David-Neel, *Magic and Mystery in Tibet*. New York: University Books, 1958, pp. 157–66. For the history of the Shijaypa, see G. N. Roerich, *Blue Annals*. Calcutta: Asiatic Soc., 1953, bks. 12, 13.

7. *blo-sbyong-brgyud*: tradition which emphasizes the development of bodhicitta. This type of mental training was developed by Atisha and is especially emphasized by his Kadampa sect and its successor, the Gelugpa.

8. See chapter 4, n. 8.

9. See *'Phags-lam*, 113/2–4.

10. See *'Phags-lam*, 113/4–6.

11. See *'Phags-lam*, 113/6–114/1.

12. It is best to recite both prayers in every session of Guru-Yoga practice. However, as both serve the same function, the meditator may recite the long prayer once daily, and the short one at subsequent sessions. (Lama)

13. See *'Phags-lam*, 114/1–116/3. This magnificent prayer consists of twenty-seven four-line verses. In each verse the name of one or more gurus is mentioned. This is followed by a description of that guru's qualities or accomplishments, in high religious language. The last line of each verse ends with the refrain, "I pray to you. Grant me co-emergent awareness!" For this term, see H. V. Guenther's *Naropa*, p. 25, n. 3.

The *gDams-ngag-mdzod* edition of *'Phags-lam* lacks the five verses of this prayer which were compiled after Kongtrul's death. For the complete list of Mahamudra gurus, see chapter 2, n. 7.

14. See *'Phags-lam*, 116/3–5.

15. See *'Phags-lam*, 116/6–117/3.

16. See *'Phags-lam*, 117/4–6. This prayer is called the "Ma-nam Four" because each line begins, "My mothers (*ma-rnams*), all sentient beings . . ."

17. See *'Phags-lam*, 117/6. "Karmapa khyen-no (*mkhyen-no*)": "Karmapa, know me, see my suffering." This is recited repeatedly, like a mantra, while visualizing or thinking about one or all of the Karmapas. If you have met His Holiness, think of him. (Lama)

18. See *'Phags-lam*, 117/6–7. This is to be recited a total of 111,111 times. After reciting it the desired number of times for the session, proceed to the next prayer. (Lama)

19. See *'Phags-lam*, 118/1–6. The six verses of this prayer are well described in Kongtrul's commentary.

Empowerment or *wong* (*dbang*) generally refers to a public ritual in which a guru confers the authority and ability to use a specific Vajrayana practice. Here, the Four Empowerments are received during private meditation, when no guru is physically present. However, according to Kalu Rinpoche, they must have previously been conferred in an external ritual. Virtually any Vajrayana empowerment ritual will accomplish this. Thus, the Avalokiteshvara or Tara empowerment also enables one to practice the Guru-Yoga.

According to Kalu Rinpoche, every empowerment has three aspects:

    a. ground (Tib. *gzhi*) : the ritual itself.

    b. path (*lam*) : meditation.

    c. result (*'bras-bu*) : ability to practice effectively and achieve the ultimate goal of the practice.

The immediate result of these Four Empowerments is the ability to. receive the Mahamudra "pointing-out" instructions, in which the guru directly demonstrates the nature of mind.

The ultimate result is realization of the nature of mind and achievement of the four Buddha-kayas, as follows:

    a. Realizing the open (*stong-pa*) nature of mind leads to the Dharmakaya.

    b. Realizing the clear (*gsal-ba*) nature of mind leads to the Sambhogakaya.

    c. Realizing the unimpeded (*ma-'gags-pa*) nature of mind leads to the Nirmanakaya.

    d. Realizing the three together leads to the Svabhavikakaya. (Kalu Rinpoche, Interview, Nov. 4, 1974).

An empowerment creates a close bond between disciple and guru, as well as between the disciple and the yidam or other enlightened being whose meditation is the subject of the empowerment. To denounce or neglect either one is a grave offense. (Lama)

20. The Vase Empowerment purifies and refines the individual, enabling him to clearly visualize the pure forms of the deities in the meditation of the Developing Stage (see below).

21. The Developing Stage (*bskyed-rim*) is the conceptual (*dmigs-bcas*) stage of a Vajrayana meditation. It is followed by the non-conceptual (*dmigs-med*) Fulfillment Stage (*rdzogs-rim*). See Beyer, *Cult of Tara,* pp. 100–43.

In the Developing Stage, the object of meditation (guru, yidam, etc.) is first visualized as present, and then visualized "in action." In the present meditation the "action" is the conferral of the Four Empowerments, symbolized by the rays of colored light flowing from the guru's form into the meditator's body.

In the Fulfillment Stage, the meditator dissolves the visualization and rests in the non-conceptual state, the experience of emptiness which occurs at the dissolution of the visualization.

According to Kalu Rinpoche, in the Developing Stage we establish wholesome thought-patterns by substituting pure, wholesome appearances and concepts for random or unwholesome ones. Since we ourselves have "produced" the visualization, we do not mistake it for something substantial or ultimately real. [We try to retain this view during all encounters with samsara's appearances.] In the Fulfillment Stage we dissolve this visualization into nothing. This can lead directly to realization of emptiness and Mahamudra. (Public lecture, Vancouver, Feb. 19, 1975).

22. *Tsa-Lung* (*rtsa-rlung*): A yogic practice in which the "pathways" (*rtsa*) and "motility" (*rlung*) are visualized within the body. See Guenther's *Naropa,* p. 46, n. 1, and pp. 158–74, 270–72.

23. Kalu Rinpoche has explained *Nyom-jug* (*snyom-'jug*: "blending of equals") meditation as follows:

> To truly receive empowerment to meditate on the blending of equals means that one is authorized and able to completely control the *rtsa, rlung* and *thig-le,* and practice *yab-yum* meditation. The latter may involve meditating on two yidams such as Cakrasamvara (symbolizing skillful means or compassion) and Vajravarahi (insight or openness) in *yab-yum* (sexual union). Alternatively, it may involve meditation on a single deity such as Cakrasamvara. In that case, one would imagine the union of the clear (*gsal-ba*) aspect of the yidam's mind, representing skillful means, with its open (*stong-pa*) aspect, representing insight. (Interview, Nov. 4, 1974).

The results of this practice include the experience of the bliss of transcending awareness (*ye-shes*) culminating in full enlightenment, Dharmakaya.

H. V. Guenther, quoting Gampopa and Padma Karpo, explains *Nyom-jug* meditation as that which involves sexual union with a *karmamudra,* or actual woman, through which the same results as above are achieved. See his *Naropa,* pp. 269–70.

24. Mental obscurations (Tib. *shes-grib*): ignorance or bewilderment. Emotional obscurations (*nyon-grib*): the conflicting emotions. Meditation-clinging obscurations (*snyom-'jug-grib*): clinging to the bliss and tranquility of samadhi. This obscures the ultimate goal—the liberation of all beings—and leads to rebirth as a god. Arhats, who perfect samadhi, are considered by Mahayanists to be especially susceptible to this type of obscuration, which entraps them in the Hinayana attitude. (Lama)

25. Three gates: body, speech and mind.

26. Mahamudra (*phyag-rgya-chen-po*): the highest goal and practice of the Kagyud sect. It is the subject of the last ten pages of our text, which have not been translated.

The theoretical basis of Mahamudra is explained by Guenther in his *Naropa,* pp. 222–35.

27. If you have great faith in him, you will now be able to visualize your own guru's form dissolving into light. Otherwise, he will simply take the form of Vajradhara. (Lama)

28. It is not possible to entirely avoid the painful results of previous acts. But the guru can hasten their fruition so that we experience them now instead of later. As human beings in contact with the Dharma and the guru, we are in a far better position to cope with adversity than we may be later on, in lower rebirths. Thus, painful experiences may be signs of the guru's compassion. (LPL)

29. When you are practicing the Guru-Yoga, it is best to make your guru the focus of all your practice. (LPL)

30. A Vajrayana or vajra-master is a teacher who has received empowerment, studied, achieved some realization and is capable of teaching the Vajrayana. (Lama)

31. Nyendrub (*bsnyen-grub*): recitation of mantras and performance of rituals concerned with a yidam. Performance of large numbers of such practices is highly regarded by the Tibetan tradition.

32. Opposite of the "profound path of the Guru-Yoga" described in this chapter, which results in the spontaneous achievement of both types of siddhi.

33. Since it is not subject to verbalization, any attempt to do so is pure distortion.

34. See chapter 1, n. 40.

35. Killing, stealing, lying and sexual misconduct.

36. Devadatta, Shakyamuni's jealous cousin, is the villain in traditional accounts of the Buddha's life. See Foucher's *Life of the Buddha*, pp. 212–14.

37. *skyes-bu dam-pa*; Skt. *satpurusha*. According to Edgerton, this denotes, ". . . a kind of lay equivalent of the Bodhisattvas," e.g., Vimalakirti.

38. See chapter 2, n. 34.

39. A guru who has not achieved realization can only offer limited help to a disciple. He cannot guide him to complete realization. (Lama)

40. *lung*: the ceremony by which a guru confers the authority to read, study and practice the teachings of a particular text. He does this by reading the text aloud very rapidly while the recipient listens. In most cases this ceremonial reading is incomprehensible. The *lung* ceremony may or may not be followed by an explanation of the text. The guru must have first himself received this authorization in a similar ceremony.

The *lung* ceremony may be a remainder of the purely oral transmission of Buddha's words which was commonly practiced before the scriptures were written down. (LPL) Seen this way, the *lung* would be a means of authenticating a text as Buddha's words.

41. I.e., think of your root-guru as essentially the same as Gampopa or any other member of the Mahamudra lineage, to which he belongs.

42. "Father" here denotes Gampopa. (LPL)

43. This is because his root-guru will then possess the qualities of Gampopa and his line.

44. *'Byams-dpal zhal-lung*: an Indian text by Buddhajnanapada (Sangs-rgyas Ye-shes), *bsTan.*, P. 2717.

According to Deshung Rinpoche, Buddhajnanapada practiced so much Manjushri meditation that Manjushri gave him this text in a vision.

45. In both verses, Vajradhara is the speaker. "Future Vajradhara" refers to the guru.

46. *sGron-ma gsal-ba. bsTan.*, P. 2650. Indian text by Candrakirti dealing with the *Guhyasamaja tantra*.

47. Your Vajrayana guru is a very significant individual (*yul-gnyan-po*) in your life. Everything you do in relation to him will have great con-

sequences, whether good or bad. Acts in relation to a Hinayana or Maha-yana teacher are not as potent. (LPL)

48. First of the fourteen "root transgressions" (*rtsa-ltung*) of the Vajrayana. Any of these destroys the sacred bond (*dam-tshig*) between you and your Vajrayana guru. The fourteen are:
1. slandering or belittling your guru
2. violating the Buddha's precepts
3. getting angry at your co-Vajrayanists
4. abandoning benevolence
5. abandoning the enlightened attitude
6. disparaging the tenets of other sects
7. publicizing secret teachings
8. having contempt for your essential Buddha-nature
9. slandering emptiness
10. befriending bad people
11. not contemplating emptiness
12. arguing with others
13. neglecting your sacred commitments
14. slandering women, who are the source of insight

See Beyer, *Cult of Tara*, p. 405. Only the first is discussed in our text.

There are also eight "branch transgressions." See *Cult of Tara*, p. 405, and J. D. Willis, *The Diamond Light*. New York: Simon and Schuster, 1973, pp. 100–106.

49. Everyone who has begun to practice Dharma has embarked on the "boat" destined for enlightenment. A spirit of love and mutual support in the face of all occurrences will help ensure a successful voyage. (Lama)

50. '*Phags-pa dad-pa'i stobs-skyed-pa la 'jug-pa phyag-rgya'i mdo. bKa'.*, P. 867.

51. Here, "Bodhisattva" signifies "guru."

52. Ngu-'bod; Skt. Raurava: one of the eight hot hells, whose name reflects the cries of pain of its inhabitants.

53. The Dharmakaya is naked (*rjen-pa*) because it is visualized with-out the ornaments and rich clothing of the Sambhoga and Nirmanakaya. This represents the fact that the Dharmakaya is utterly beyond samsara, and cannot be characterized in terms drawn from samsara.

54. Many rituals for prolonging life focus upon the Buddha Amitayus or the yidam Tara. See Beyer, *Cult of Tara*, pp. 363–98.

55. Bhaishajyaguru (Tib. sMan-bla, pronounced "Menla") is the "Medicine Buddha" invoked in rituals of healing.

In this section, Kongtrul is urging us to see the guru as the Buddha and to choose from the great variety of Buddha-symbols the one which is the most personally meaningful. The spiritually advanced may regard the guru as the Dharmakaya; ordinary persons will regard him as the Buddha-symbol closest to their interests, e.g., long life, wealth, and so on.

56. The guru is called "Lord of the Mandala" because 1. the guru leads his disciple through the mandala (chilkor, see chap. 3, n. 20) prac-tice, acquainting him with all its symbols of enlightenment; 2. the guru is considered non-separate from the "Principal One," the central symbol of

enlightenment in the mandala who stands for the integration of all the surrounding figures. (LPL)

57. Jayulpa (Bya-yul-pa): an eleventh-century Kadampa teacher.
(LPL)

58. See n. 44 above.

59. Kongtrul is urging us to eliminate the three conflicting emotions:
attachment (expectation of reward), aversion (fear of punishment or dis-
appointment) and bewilderment (not caring). We are asked to transform
bewilderment into devotion and reverence, without being motivated by
attachment or aversion.

60. *dag-snang*: seeing things accurately, without imposing value-
judgements. Guenther calls this "aesthetic immediacy, pure and uncon-
taminated." See his *Tantric View of Life*. Berkeley: Shambhala, 1972, pp.
27–8.

COLOPHON

This was written at the request of Jetsun Lama Karma Odsal Gyurme,
who desired an easily read, complete and clear description of the visualizations and explanation of the Four Foundations of Mahamudra. It is a
supplementary text to the ninth Karmapa's *Ocean of Certainty*.[1]

I myself have achieved no realization and make no false claims to
originality but have based this work on the sayings of the great ones.

—Written by the false renunciate[2] Karma Ngawong Yontan Gyatso,
age thirty-one, at the Kunzang Dechen retreat center of Palpung monastery. May it serve to spread the teachings! May its merit be shared by all!

NOTES

1. *Nges-don rgya-mtsho.*
2. *spong-ba-pa'i zol-can*: traditional term of self-denigration.

Bibliography

PRIMARY SOURCES

dBang-phyug rDorje, Karmapa IX, and others. *sGrub-brgyud Karma Kam-tshang-pa'i phyag-chen lhan-cig skyes-sbyor-gyi sngon-'gro bzhi-sbyor sogs-kyi ngag-'don 'phags-lam bgrod-pa'i shing-rta: Karma Kam-tshang sngon-'gro. gDams-ngag-mdzod,* vol. 6, fols. 105–22. Delhi: N. Lungtok and N. Gyaltsan, 1971.

_____. *Phyag-rgya-chen-po lhan-cig skyes-sbyor-gyi khrid-ki spyi-sdom rtsa-tshig. gDams-ngag-mdzod,* vol. 6, fols. 62–69. Delhi: N. Lungtok and N. Gyaltsan, 1971.

_____. *Phyag-rgya-chen-po lhan-cig skyes-sbyor-gyi khrid zin-bris snying-po gsal-ba'i sgron-me bdud-rtsi'i nying-khu chos-sku mdzub-tshugs su ngo-sprod-pa: Karma Kam-tshang phyag-chen. gDams-ngag-mdzod,* vol. 6, fols. 70–104. Delhi: N. Lungtok and N. Gyaltsan, 1971.

Chang, G. C. C., trans. and annot. *The Hundred Thousand Songs of Mila-repa.* New York: University Books, 1962.

Evans-Wentz, W. Y., ed. *Tibet's Great Yogi Milarepa.* New York: Oxford University Press, 1957.

Fremantle, F., and Trungpa, C., trans. and commen. *The Tibetan Book of the Dead: The Great Liberation through Hearing in the Bardo.* Berke-ley: Shambhala, 1975.

Guenther, H. V., trans. and annot. *The Jewel Ornament of Liberation by sGam-po-pa.* Berkeley: Shambhala, 1959.

_____, trans. and commen. *The Life and Teaching of Naropa.* New York: Oxford University Press, 1963.

_____, trans. and annot. *The Royal Song of Saraha.* Seattle: University of Washington Press, 1969.

'Jam-mgon Kong-sprul blo-gros mtha'-yas-pa. *Phyag-chen sngon-'gro bzhi-sbyor dang dngos-gzhi'i khrid-rim mdor-bsdus nges-don sgron-me.* dPal-spungs edition, 1844.

La Vallée Poussin, L. de. "L'Abhidharmakosa de Vasubandhu," *Mélanges Chinois et Bouddhiques,* vol. 16. Bruxelles: Institut Belge Des Hautes Études Chinoises, 1971.

_____, trans. and annot. *Vijnaptimatratasiddhi: la siddhi de Hiuan-tsang.* Paris: Paul Geuthner, 1928-29.

Lokesh Chandra and Raghu Vira, eds. *Kalacakra-tantra and Other Texts.*

Sata-pitaka series, vols. 69–70. New Delhi: International Academy of
Indian Culture, 1966.

McLeod, I., trans. *Foundational Practices: Excerpts from The Chariot for
Travelling the Supreme Path by the Ninth Karmapa dBang-phyug
rDorje.* Vancouver: Kagyu Kunkhyab Chuling, 1976.

McLeod, K., trans. *A Direct Path to Enlightenment* [*Theg-pa chen-po blo-
sbyong don bdun-ma'i khrid-yig blo-dman 'jug bder bkod-pa byang-
chub gzhung-lam*], by 'Jam-mgon Kong-sprul. Vancouver: Kagyu
Kunkhyab Chuling, 1974.

_____. *Writings of Kalu Rinpoche.* Vancouver: Kagyu Kunkhyab Chu-
ling, 1976.

Matics, M., trans. *Entering the Path of Enlightenment: the Bodhicarya-
avatara of the Buddhist poet Santideva.* New York: Macmillan, 1970.

Obermiller, E., trans. *Bu-ston's History of Buddhism.* Heidelberg: Materie-
len zur Kunde des Buddhismus, 1931-32.

Roerich, G. N., trans. and annot. *The Blue Annals: the Stages of the Appearance of the Doctrine and Preachers in the Land of Tibet.* 2 vols.
Calcutta: Royal Asiatic Society, 1949 and 1953.

Ruegg, D. S., trans. and annot. *The Life of Bu-ston Rin-po-che.* Rome Oriental Series, no. 34. Roma: Instituto italiano per il Medio ed Estremo
oriente, 1966.

Stein, R. A., trans. and annot. *Vie et chants de 'Brug-pa Kun-legs le yogin.*
Paris: G. P. Maisonneuve et Larose, 1972.

SECONDARY SOURCES

BOOKS

Beyer, S. *The Cult of Tara: Magic and Ritual in Tibet.* Berkeley: University
of California Press, 1973.

Bhattacaryya, B. *The Indian Buddhist Iconography.* Calcutta: Firma Muk-
hopadhyay, 1958.

Blofeld, J. *The Tantric Mysticism of Tibet.* New York: Causeway, 1974.

Chang, G. C. C. *The Buddhist Teaching of Totality: The Philosophy of
Hwa-Yen Buddhism.* Pittsburgh: Pennsylvania State University Press,
1971.

Clark, W. E. *Two Lamaistic Pantheons.* New York: Paragon, 1965.

Dasgupta, S. B. *An Introduction to Tantric Buddhism.* 2nd ed. Berkeley:
Shambhala, 1974.

David-Neel, A. *Magic and Mystery in Tibet.* New York: University Books,
1958.

Eliade, M. *Shamanism: Archaic Techniques of Ecstasy.* London: Routledge
and Kegan Paul, 1964.

Eracle, J. *L'Art des thanka et le bouddhisme tantrique.* Genève: Musée d'ethnographie, 1970.

Foucher, A. *The Life of the Buddha.* Abridged translation by Simone B. Boas. Middletown, Conn.: Wesleyan University Press, 1963.

Getty, A. *The Gods of Northern Buddhism.* 2nd ed. Rutland, Vermont: Tuttle, 1962.

Guenther, H. V. *Buddhist Philosophy in Theory and Practice.* Baltimore: Penguin, 1972.

_____. *The Tantric View of Life.* Berkeley: Shambhala, 1972.

_____. *Treasures on the Tibetan Middle Way.* Berkeley: Shambhala, 1971.

Lessing, F. D. *Yung-ho-kung: An Iconography of the Lamaist Cathedral in Peking.* Reports from the Scientific Expedition to the Northwestern Provinces of China under the leadership of Dr. Sven Hedin, pt. 8, vol. 1. Stockholm, 1942.

Ling, T. O. *Buddhism and the Mythology of Evil.* London: Allen and Unwin, 1962.

Matsunaga, D. and A. *The Buddhist Concept of Hell.* New York: Philosophical Library, 1972.

Nebesky-Wojkowitz, R. *Oracles and Demons of Tibet.* S'Gravenhage: Mouton, 1956.

Ruegg, D. S. *Théorie du tathagatagarbha et du gotra.* Paris: Ecole Francaise D'Extrême-Orient, 1969.

Schmid, T. *The Eighty-Five Siddhas.* Reports from the Scientific Expedition to the Northwestern Provinces of China under the leadership of Dr. Sven Hedin, pt. 8, vol. 7. Stockholm, 1958.

Shakabpa, W. B. *Tibet—A Political History.* New Haven: Yale University Press, 1967.

Stein, R. A. *Tibetan Civilization.* Translated by J. E. Stapleton Driver. London: Faber and Faber, 1972.

Tucci, G. *Tibetan Painted Scrolls.* Roma: La Libreria Dello Stato, 1949.

Wayman, A. *The Buddhist Tantras.* New York: Samuel Weiser, 1973.

Willis, J. D. *The Diamond Light: an Introduction to Tibetan Buddhist Meditations.* New York: Simon and Schuster, 1973.

Zimmer, H. *Philosophies of India.* Princeton: Bollingen, 1951.

ARTICLES

Bloss, L. W. "The Buddha and the Naga: A Study in Buddhist Folk Religiosity," *History of Religions* 13, no. 1: 36–53.

Lessing, F. D. "Miscellaneous Lamaist Notes I: Notes on the Thanksgiving Offering," *Central Asiatic Journal* 2, no. 1: 58–71.

Li-An-Che. "The bKa'-brgyud sect of Lamaism," *Journal of the American Oriental Society* 69, no. 2: 51–59.

Richardson, H. E. "The Karma-pa sect: a historical note," *Journal of the Royal Asiatic Society*, 1958: 139–64; 1959: 1–17.

Schubert, J. "Das Reis-Mandala," *Asiatica, Festschrift Friedrich Weller*, 1954: 584–609.

Smith, G. "Introduction," to the *Ses-bya Kun-khyab*, Lokesh Chandra, ed., Sata-pitaka series, 80. New Delhi: International Academy of Indian Culture, 1970: 1–87.

Wylie, T. "Ro-langs: the Tibetan Zombie," *History of Religions* 4, no. 1: 69–80.

Index 1: General Names and Subjects

Index 2: Tibetan Technical Terms and Names